# RISING STARS
# Mathematics

Year
# 3

## Practice Book

Author: Paul Broadbent

ISBN: 978-1-78339-816-4
Text, design and layout © Rising Stars UK Ltd 2016

First published in 2015 by
Rising Stars UK Ltd, part of Hodder Education,
An Hachette UK Company
Carmelite House
50 Victoria Embankment
London EC4Y 0DZ
www.risingstars-uk.com

Author: Paul Broadbent
Programme consultants: Caroline Clissold, Cherri Moseley, Paul Broadbent
Publishers: Fiona Lazenby and Alexandra Riley
Editorial: Jan Fisher, Aidan Gill
Answer checker, Deborah Dobson
Project manager: Sue Walton

Series and character design: Steve Evans
Typesetting and illustration: Steve Evans

Cover design: Steve Evans and Words & Pictures
Printed by Liberduplex, Barcelona
A catalogue record for this title is available from the British Library.

# Contents

# Unit 1 — All about numbers

**1** Use Base 10 apparatus to help complete the sentences.

**YOU WILL NEED:**
• Base 10 apparatus

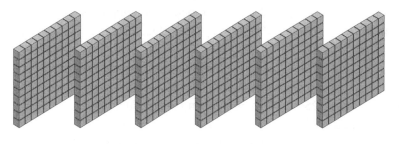

a   10 more than 628 is [ ]

c   100 more than 628 is [ ]

b   10 less than 628 is [ ]

d   100 less than 628 is [ ]

**2** Now show the numbers by drawing beads on each abacus.

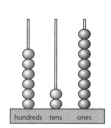

a   10 more than 628 is [ ]

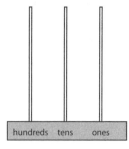

c   100 more than 628 is [ ]

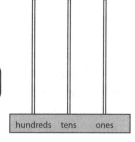

b   10 less than 628 is [ ]

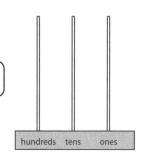

d   100 less than 628 is [ ]

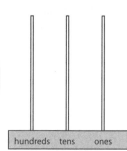

**3** Look at these patterns. Write the next 3 numbers.

a   410   510   610   [   ]   [   ]   [   ]

b   120   130   140   [   ]   [   ]   [   ]

c   126   226   326   [   ]   [   ]   [   ]

d   485   495   505   [   ]   [   ]   [   ]

e   692   682   672   [   ]   [   ]   [   ]

f   789   689   589   [   ]   [   ]   [   ]

**4** Count in these steps. Write the missing numbers.

a   Count in 10s  ➜  472   [   ]   [   ]   [   ]   512

b   Count in 10s  ➜  408   [   ]   [   ]   [   ]   448

c   Count in 100s  ➜  359   [   ]   [   ]   [   ]   759

d   Count in 100s  ➜  623   [   ]   [   ]   [   ]   1023

**5**

**YOU WILL NEED:**
• a ruler

Use a ruler to measure the length of each line accurately in centimetres.
Complete the table to show each length in centimetres (cm) and in millimetres (mm).

a ▬▬▬▬▬▬▬

b ▬▬▬▬▬

c ▬▬▬▬▬▬▬▬▬▬▬

d ▬▬▬▬▬▬▬▬▬▬▬▬▬▬

e ▬▬▬▬▬▬▬▬▬▬▬

| Line | cm | mm |
|------|----|----|
| a | | |
| b | | |
| c | | |
| d | | |
| e | | |

**6** If you start at 911 and count on in 10s, will the number 1001 be in your counting pattern?
How can you prove it?

_____

_____

**1** Write the numbers shown by the Base 10 apparatus.

| Hundreds | Tens | Ones |
|----------|------|------|
|          |      |      |
| 1        | 5    | 4    |

$$\boxed{100} + \boxed{50} + \boxed{4} = \boxed{154}$$

**a**

| Hundreds | Tens | Ones |
|----------|------|------|
|          |      |      |
|          |      |      |

$\boxed{\phantom{0}} + \boxed{\phantom{0}} + \boxed{\phantom{0}} = \boxed{\phantom{0}}$

**d**

| Hundreds | Tens | Ones |
|----------|------|------|
|          |      |      |
|          |      |      |

$\boxed{\phantom{0}} + \boxed{\phantom{0}} + \boxed{\phantom{0}} = \boxed{\phantom{0}}$

**b**

| Hundreds | Tens | Ones |
|----------|------|------|
|          |      |      |
|          |      |      |

$\boxed{\phantom{0}} + \boxed{\phantom{0}} + \boxed{\phantom{0}} = \boxed{\phantom{0}}$

**e**

| Hundreds | Tens | Ones |
|----------|------|------|
|          |      |      |
|          |      |      |

$\boxed{\phantom{0}} + \boxed{\phantom{0}} + \boxed{\phantom{0}} = \boxed{\phantom{0}}$

**c**

| Hundreds | Tens | Ones |
|----------|------|------|
|          |      |      |
|          |      |      |

$\boxed{\phantom{0}} + \boxed{\phantom{0}} + \boxed{\phantom{0}} = \boxed{\phantom{0}}$

**f**

| Hundreds | Tens | Ones |
|----------|------|------|
|          |      |      |
|          |      |      |

$\boxed{\phantom{0}} + \boxed{\phantom{0}} + \boxed{\phantom{0}} = \boxed{\phantom{0}}$

Use place-value cards to help you make these numbers.

a

b

c

d

e

f

**3** Draw beads on each abacus to show these numbers.

**a** 361

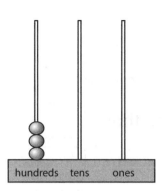

hundreds tens ones

**d** 910

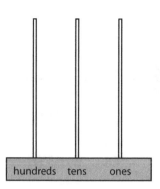

hundreds tens ones

**b** 244

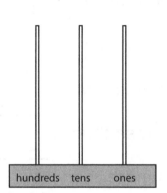

hundreds tens ones

**e** 523

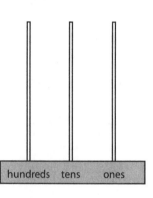

hundreds tens ones

**c** 703

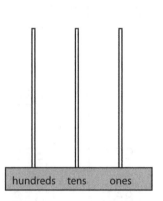

hundreds tens ones

**f** 811

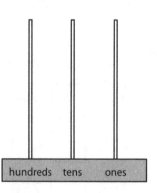

hundreds tens ones

What do you notice about the number of beads on each abacus?

 **4** How many 3-digit numbers can you make from the digits 1, 2 and 3?

Make a list of the numbers. Write them in order starting with the smallest.

_____

**1** Complete each sentence. Write the two numbers in the correct place.

a   47   83   [   ] is less than [   ]

b   74   79   [   ] is less than [   ]

c   55   56   [   ] is more than [   ]

d   81   29   [   ] is more than [   ]

e   347   383   [   ] is less than [   ]

f   474   479   [   ] is less than [   ]

g   755   756   [   ] is more than [   ]

h   881   829   [   ] is more than [   ]

**2** Write in the missing < or > sign for each pair of numbers.

a   347 [   ] 383          e   247 [   ] 483

b   474 [   ] 479          f   574 [   ] 379

c   755 [   ] 756          g   855 [   ] 656

d   881 [   ] 829          h   781 [   ] 929

**3** Circle the larger mass in each pair.

a   35 g   53 g          e   415 g   614 g

b   135 g   153 g          f   416 g   414 g

c   531 g   351 g          g   565 g   656 g

d   315 g   513 g          h   775 g   757 g

**4** Write each group in order starting with the smallest.

**a**

241 ml    240 ml    248 ml    246 ml

☐ ☐ ☐ ☐

**Smallest**

**b**

375 ml    175 ml    275 ml    475 ml

☐ ☐ ☐ ☐

**Smallest**

**c**

469 ml    439 ml    489 ml    419 ml

☐ ☐ ☐ ☐

**Smallest**

**d**

512 ml    521 ml    251 ml    215 ml

☐ ☐ ☐ ☐

**Smallest**

**e**

765 ml    432 ml    987 ml    654 ml

☐ ☐ ☐ ☐

**Smallest**

**f**

849 ml    893 ml    709 ml    757 ml

☐ ☐ ☐ ☐

**Smallest**

Use 3 counters to cover squares on the number grid for these activities.

| 100 | 200 | 300 | 400 | 500 | 600 | 700 | 800 | 900 |
|-----|-----|-----|-----|-----|-----|-----|-----|-----|
| 10 | 20 | 30 | 40 | 50 | 60 | 70 | 80 | 90 |
| 1 | 2 | 3 | 4 | 5 | 6 | 7 | 8 | 9 |

**5**   Place the 3 counters in different squares down the grid.
**Only one counter is allowed in each row and each column.**
Explore the different numbers you can make.

a   Which is the largest number you can make?

b   Which is the smallest number you can make
with 3 counters?

c   Which is the nearest number to 500 that you can
make with 3 counters?

**6**   Arrange the counters on the grid to make possible missing numbers for each of these.
Record one number for each.

a   429 > ⬚ > 421

b   647 < ⬚ < 657

c   285 > ⬚ > 185

d   333 < ⬚ < 444

**1** Write the number at each arrow.

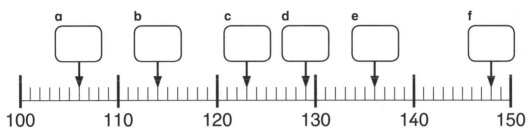

**2** Write the number at each arrow.

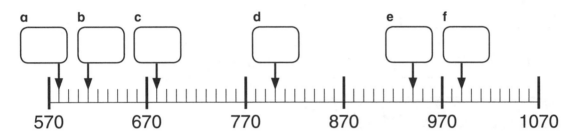

**3** Write the value of each of these in pence.

a         p

b         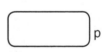 p

c           p

d           p

**4** Write the numbers shown by the Base 10 apparatus.

**a**

| Hundreds | Tens | Ones |
|---|---|---|

⬚ hundreds ⬚ tens ⬚ ones ➜ ⬚

**b**

| Hundreds | Tens | Ones |
|---|---|---|

⬚ hundreds ⬚ tens ⬚ ones ➜ ⬚

**c**

| Hundreds | Tens | Ones |
|---|---|---|

⬚ hundreds ⬚ tens ⬚ ones ➜ ⬚

**d**

| Hundreds | Tens | Ones |
|---|---|---|

⬚ hundreds ⬚ tens ⬚ ones ➜ ⬚

**e**

| Hundreds | Tens | Ones |
|---|---|---|

⬚ hundreds ⬚ tens ⬚ ones ➜ ⬚

**5** Write the value of the missing place-value card for each of these.

**a** 386

**b** 239

**c** 684

**d** 719

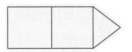  

**e** 969

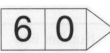 

**f** 551

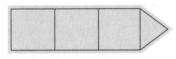

**6** Show these numbers in 4 different ways.

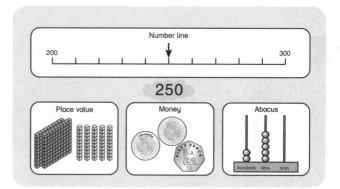

**a**

### Number line

**350**

| Place value | Money | Abacus |
|---|---|---|

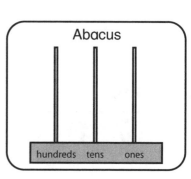

**b**

### Number line

**345**

| Place value | Money | Abacus |
|---|---|---|

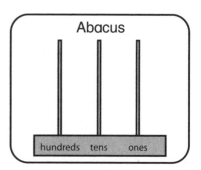

c

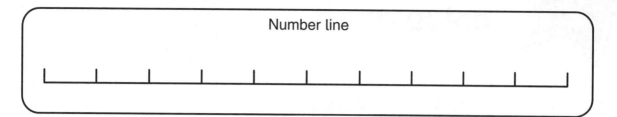

Number line

425

Place value

Money

Abacus

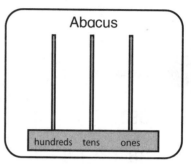

hundreds   tens   ones

7

YOU WILL NEED:
• counters

This abacus has 4 beads on it.
It shows the number 202.

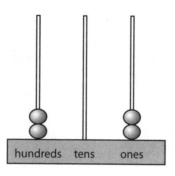

hundreds   tens   ones

What other numbers can you make with 4 beads?

Place counters on the abacus to make the numbers.
Record them in the box.

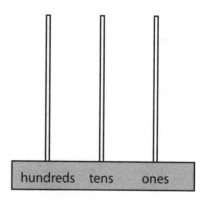

hundreds   tens   ones

**1** Complete these.

a   38 + 7  = ☐

   38 + **2** + **5** = ☐

b   36 + 9 = ☐

   36 + **4** + **5** = ☐

c   45 + 8 = ☐

   45 + **5** + **3** = ☐

d   57 + 6 = ☐

   57 + **3** + **3** = ☐

e   59 + 8 = ☐

   ☐ + ☐ + ☐ = ☐

f   63 + 9 = ☐

   ☐ + ☐ + ☐ = ☐

 **2** Complete these.

a   34 − 7  = ☐

   34 − **4** − **3** = ☐

b   36 − 8 = ☐

   36 − **6** − **2** = ☐

c   25 − 8 = ☐

   25 − **5** − **3** = ☐

d   47 − 9 = ☐

   47 − **7** − **2** = ☐

e   52 − 7 = ☐

   ☐ − ☐ − ☐ = ☐

f   64 − 9 = ☐

   ☐ − ☐ − ☐ = ☐

**3** Answer these. Use the strategy of rounding and adjusting.

**a**

$46 + 9 = 46 + \boxed{10} - 1 = \boxed{55}$

$46 + 19 = 46 + \boxed{\phantom{0}} - 1 = \boxed{\phantom{0}}$

$46 + 29 = 46 + \boxed{\phantom{0}} - 1 = \boxed{\phantom{0}}$

$46 + 39 = 46 + \boxed{\phantom{0}} - 1 = \boxed{\phantom{0}}$

**c**

$58 - 9 = 58 - \boxed{10} + 1 = \boxed{49}$

$58 - 19 = 58 - \boxed{\phantom{0}} + 1 = \boxed{\phantom{0}}$

$58 - 29 = 58 - \boxed{\phantom{0}} + 1 = \boxed{\phantom{0}}$

$58 - 39 = 58 - \boxed{\phantom{0}} + 1 = \boxed{\phantom{0}}$

**b**

$54 + 8 = 54 + \boxed{10} - 2 = \boxed{62}$

$54 + 18 = 54 + \boxed{\phantom{0}} - 2 = \boxed{\phantom{0}}$

$54 + 28 = 54 + \boxed{\phantom{0}} - 2 = \boxed{\phantom{0}}$

$54 + 38 = 54 + \boxed{\phantom{0}} - 2 = \boxed{\phantom{0}}$

**d**

$63 - 8 = 63 - \boxed{10} + 2 = \boxed{55}$

$63 - 18 = 63 - \boxed{\phantom{0}} + 2 = \boxed{\phantom{0}}$

$63 - 28 = 63 - \boxed{\phantom{0}} + 2 = \boxed{\phantom{0}}$

$63 - 38 = 63 - \boxed{\phantom{0}} + 2 = \boxed{\phantom{0}}$

 **4** Circle the number on the line that is the nearest 10 for the number given.
Use this to help answer the 2 calculations by rounding.
Check carefully on the number line to see if you add or subtract the extra.

**a** 39

30 |⌐ _ _ _ _ _ _ _ _ _ ⌐| 40

$45 + 39 = \boxed{\phantom{0}}$    $45 - 39 = \boxed{\phantom{0}}$

**b** 28

20 |⌐ _ _ _ _ _ _ _ _ _ ⌐| 30

$63 + 28 = \boxed{\phantom{0}}$    $63 - 28 = \boxed{\phantom{0}}$

**c** 38

30 |⌐ _ _ _ _ _ _ _ _ _ ⌐| 40

$53 + 38 = \boxed{\phantom{0}}$    $53 - 38 = \boxed{\phantom{0}}$

**d** 47

40 |⌐ _ _ _ _ _ _ _ _ _ ⌐| 50

$52 + 47 = \boxed{\phantom{0}}$    $52 - 47 = \boxed{\phantom{0}}$

**5** Answer these. Partition to help work out your answer.

**a**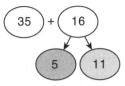

35 + 16 = ☐

**b**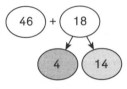

46 + 18 = ☐

**c**

57 + 15 = ☐

**d**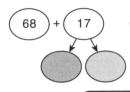

68 + 17 = ☐

**e**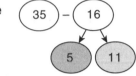

35 − 16 = ☐

**f**

46 − 18 = ☐

**g**

57 − 15 = ☐

**h**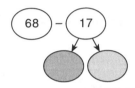

68 − 17 = ☐

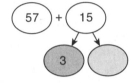
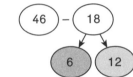

My mother is 37.

**6** Read and answer these.

**a** My aunt is 9 years older than my mother. How old is my aunt? ☐

**b** My grandfather is 28 years older than my mother. How old is my grandfather? ☐

**c** My father is 8 years younger than my aunt. How old is my father? ☐

**d** My uncle is 7 years older than my father. How old is my uncle? ☐

**e** My grandmother was 25 when my mother was born. How old is my grandmother? ☐

**f** My great-grandmother is 48 years older than my mother. How old is my great-grandmother? ☐

⭐ **7** Try these 'think of a number' problems. Decide on a mental strategy to answer them.

**a** I'm thinking of a number. If I add 9 to it the answer is 14.
What is my number?

**b** I'm thinking of a number. If I subtract 18 from it the answer is 24.
What is my number?

**c** I'm thinking of a number. If I add 22 to it the answer is 40.
What is my number?

**d** I'm thinking of a number. If I take away 26 from it the answer is 41.
What is my number?

Make up your own 'think of a number' problems like these.

⭐ **8** Look at these calculations:

**a** Write a digit in each box so that the calculation is correct.
Which other ways can you do it?
What patterns do you notice?

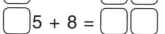

☐5 + 8 = ☐☐
☐5 + 8 = ☐☐
☐5 + 8 = ☐☐
☐5 + 8 = ☐☐
☐5 + 8 = ☐☐
☐5 + 8 = ☐☐

Working

**b** Write a digit in each box so that the calculation is correct.
Which other ways can you do it?
What patterns do you notice?

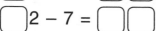
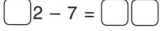

☐2 − 7 = ☐☐
☐2 − 7 = ☐☐
☐2 − 7 = ☐☐
☐2 − 7 = ☐☐
☐2 − 7 = ☐☐
☐2 − 7 = ☐☐

Working

**1**  The three outside numbers total the centre number.
Write the centre numbers.

a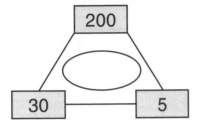

c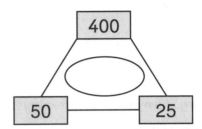

b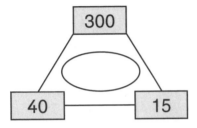

d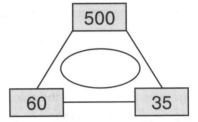

 **2**  Add these. Write the answer.

a  367 + 28

| 300 | + | 60 | + | 7 |
|-----|---|----|---|---|
|  | + | 20 | + | 8 |

☐ + ☐ + ☐ = ☐

b  209 + 179

| 200 | + | 0 | + | 9 |
|-----|---|---|---|---|
| 100 | + | 70 | + | 9 |

☐ + ☐ + ☐ = ☐

c  254 + 327

| 200 | + | 50 | + | 4 |
|-----|---|----|---|---|
| 300 | + | 20 | + | 7 |

☐ + ☐ + ☐ = ☐

d  346 + 285

| 300 | + | 40 | + | 6 |
|-----|---|----|---|---|
| 200 | + | 80 | + | 5 |

☐ + ☐ + ☐ = ☐

**3** Answer these.

**a**
```
    1  4  3
  + 3  8  7
  ┌─────────┐
  │         │
  └─────────┘
```

**c**
```
    5  3  8
  + 2  5  8
  ┌─────────┐
  │         │
  └─────────┘
```

**b**
```
    2  4  5
  + 1  2  9
  ┌─────────┐
  │         │
  └─────────┘
```

**d**
```
    3  9  6
  + 4  3  5
  ┌─────────┐
  │         │
  └─────────┘
```

 **4** Use Base 10 apparatus to subtract 135 from each of these.

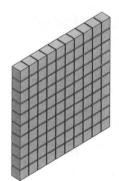 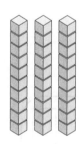 

**a** $247 - 135 = \boxed{\phantom{000}}$

**b** $232 - 135 = \boxed{\phantom{000}}$

**c** $319 - 135 = \boxed{\phantom{000}}$

**d** $304 - 135 = \boxed{\phantom{000}}$

Which did you find the most difficult ones to answer?
Why?

**5** Read and answer these.

**a** 2 buses take children on a school trip. One bus has 38 children and the other has 53 children. How many children are there in total on this school trip?

**b** A farmer has 44 chickens, 29 are white and the rest are brown. How many chickens are brown?

**c** Entrance to a theme park costs £26 for an adult. How much will it cost for 2 adults?

£

**d** A child's ticket to the theme park costs £9 less than the cost of £26 for an adult ticket. What is the price of a child's ticket to the theme park?

£

**e** A fruit drink is made with 55 ml of mango juice and 135 ml of orange juice. How much juice is there in total?

ml

**f** A piece of rope is 172 cm long and 48 cm is cut off. What is the length of the rope now?

cm

**6** Look at the jugs and answer these.

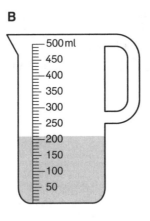 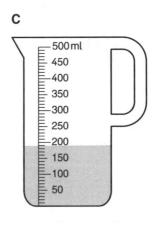 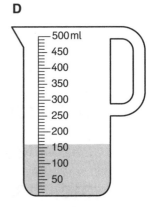

A

| 500 ml |
| 450 |
| 400 |
| 350 |
| 300 |
| 250 |
| 200 |
| 150 |
| 100 |
| 50 |

B

| 500 ml |
| 450 |
| 400 |
| 350 |
| 300 |
| 250 |
| 200 |
| 150 |
| 100 |
| 50 |

C

| 500 ml |
| 450 |
| 400 |
| 350 |
| 300 |
| 250 |
| 200 |
| 150 |
| 100 |
| 50 |

D

| 500 ml |
| 450 |
| 400 |
| 350 |
| 300 |
| 250 |
| 200 |
| 150 |
| 100 |
| 50 |

**a** Which 2 jugs total exactly 500 ml?

**b** Which jug has 50 ml less than jug B?

**c** Which 2 jugs total 400 ml?

**d** Which 2 jugs have a difference of 150 ml?

**3a**  2s, 4s and 8s

 **1**  Complete these.

| | | |
|---|---|---|
| 2 × 1 = ☐ | 4 × 1 = ☐ | 8 × 1 = ☐ |
| 2 × 2 = ☐ | 4 × 2 = ☐ | 8 × 2 = ☐ |
| 2 × 3 = ☐ | 4 × 3 = ☐ | 8 × 3 = ☐ |
| 2 × 4 = ☐ | 4 × 4 = ☐ | 8 × 4 = ☐ |
| 2 × 5 = ☐ | 4 × 5 = ☐ | 8 × 5 = ☐ |
| 2 × 6 = ☐ | 4 × 6 = ☐ | 8 × 6 = ☐ |
| 2 × 7 = ☐ | 4 × 7 = ☐ | 8 × 7 = ☐ |
| 2 × 8 = ☐ | 4 × 8 = ☐ | 8 × 8 = ☐ |
| 2 × 9 = ☐ | 4 × 9 = ☐ | 8 × 9 = ☐ |
| 2 × 10 = ☐ | 4 × 10 = ☐ | 8 × 10 = ☐ |
| 2 × 11 = ☐ | 4 × 11 = ☐ | 8 × 11 = ☐ |
| 2 × 12 = ☐ | 4 × 12 = ☐ | 8 × 12 = ☐ |

What do you notice about the answers on each line?

**2** Answer each set of calculations.

Use the first answer to help with the others in each set.

**a**

4 × 3 = 12

12 ÷ 3 = ☐    12 ÷ 4 = ☐

**d**

8 × 9 = 72

72 ÷ 9 = ☐    72 ÷ 8 = ☐

**b**

4 × 6 = 24

24 ÷ 6 = ☐    24 ÷ 4 = ☐

**e**

4 × 9 = 36

36 ÷ 9 = ☐    36 ÷ 4 = ☐

**c**

8 × 6 = 48

48 ÷ 6 = ☐    48 ÷ 8 = ☐

**f**

8 × 3 = 24

24 ÷ 3 = ☐    24 ÷ 8 = ☐

**3** Complete these facts for each triangle diagram.

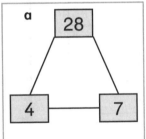

**a**

28

4 — 7

4 × ☐ = 28

☐ × 4 = 28

28 ÷ 4 = ☐

28 ÷ ☐ = 4

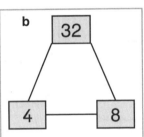

**b**

32

4 — 8

4 × ☐ = ☐

☐ × 4 = ☐

☐ ÷ 4 = ☐

☐ ÷ ☐ = 4

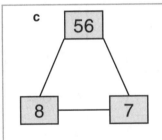

**c**

56

8 — 7

☐ × ☐ = ☐

☐ × ☐ = ☐

☐ ÷ ☐ = ☐

☐ ÷ ☐ = ☐

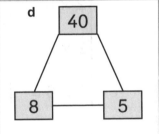

**d**

40

8 — 5

☐ × ☐ = ☐

☐ × ☐ = ☐

☐ ÷ ☐ = ☐

☐ ÷ ☐ = ☐

**4**  Look at these number machines. Complete each chart.

**a**

IN          OUT

| IN | 2 | | 8 | | 9 | |
|---|---|---|---|---|---|---|
| OUT | | 16 | | 48 | | 24 |

**b**

IN          OUT

| IN | 2 | | 8 | | 9 | |
|---|---|---|---|---|---|---|
| OUT | | 32 | | 96 | | 48 |

**5**  This pictogram shows the different types of pizzas sold in a day.

 = 4

| Type of Pizza | |
|---|---|
| Cheese | 🍕🍕🍕🍕🍕🍕🍕🍕 |
| Sweetcorn | 🍕🍕🍕🍕🍕 |
| Mushroom | 🍕🍕🍕 |
| Chicken tikka | 🍕🍕🍕🍕🍕🍕🍕 |

Use the pictogram to answer these.

**a**  Which type of pizza sold most?

**b**  For which type of pizza were 28 sold?

**c**  How many sweetcorn pizzas were sold?

**d**  How many mushroom pizzas were sold?

**e**  How many more cheese pizzas were sold than sweetcorn pizzas?

**f**  How many sweetcorn and mushroom pizzas were sold altogether?

**6** A special vegetable pizza has 2 pieces of green pepper and 4 pieces of red pepper on it.

Some vegetable pizzas were made and used 36 pieces of pepper altogether.

a How many vegetable pizzas were made?

b How many pieces of green pepper and how many pieces of red pepper were used?

pieces of green pepper

pieces of red pepper

**1** Write multiplications to match each of these.

**a**

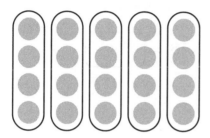

$5 \times 4 =$ ☐

**b**

☐ $\times$ ☐ $=$ ☐

**c**

☐ $\times$ ☐ $=$ ☐

**d**

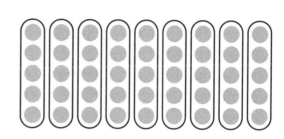

☐ $\times$ ☐ $=$ ☐

**e**

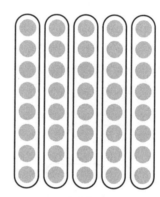

☐ $\times$ ☐ $=$ ☐

**f**

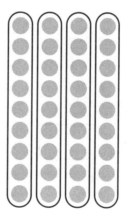

☐ $\times$ ☐ $=$ ☐

**2**    Group these to show the multiplications.

**a**

$6 \times 4 =$ ☐          $4 \times 6 =$ ☐

**b**

$8 \times 2 =$ ☐          $2 \times 8 =$ ☐

**c**

$4 \times 8 =$ ☐          $8 \times 4 =$ ☐

**d**

$6 \times 3 =$ ☐          $3 \times 6 =$ ☐

e

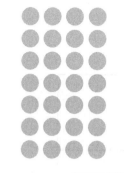

$4 \times 7 = \boxed{\phantom{00}}$

$7 \times 4 = \boxed{\phantom{00}}$

f

$7 \times 3 = \boxed{\phantom{00}}$

$3 \times 7 = \boxed{\phantom{00}}$

**3** Answer these.

a   $3 \times 4 = \boxed{\phantom{00}}$

    $4 \times 3 = \boxed{\phantom{00}}$

b   $8 \times 5 = \boxed{\phantom{00}}$

    $5 \times 8 = \boxed{\phantom{00}}$

c   $12 \times 3 = \boxed{\phantom{00}}$

    $3 \times 12 = \boxed{\phantom{00}}$

d   $4 \times 10 = \boxed{\phantom{00}}$

    $10 \times 4 = \boxed{\phantom{00}}$

e   $2 \times 7 = \boxed{\phantom{00}}$

    $7 \times 2 = \boxed{\phantom{00}}$

f   $3 \times 8 = \boxed{\phantom{00}}$

    $8 \times 3 = \boxed{\phantom{00}}$

**4** Complete this multiplication grid.

| × | 4 | | |
|---|---|---|---|
| 8 | | | 24 |
| | 16 | | 12 |
| 5 | | 10 | |

 **5** Some birds have made nests in a large tree. 2 of the nests have 5 eggs in them.
The other nests have 3 eggs in them.
There are 25 eggs altogether. How many nests have 3 eggs in them?

**1** Each set has been shared between 4 people. How many does each person get?

a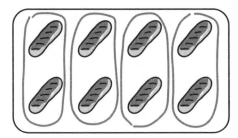

$\frac{1}{4}$ of 8 is ▢

c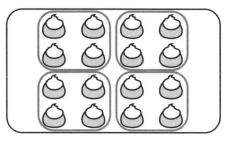

$\frac{1}{4}$ of 16 is ▢

b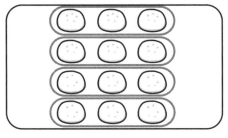

$\frac{1}{4}$ of 12 is ▢

d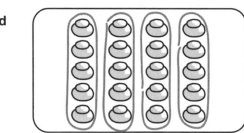

$\frac{1}{4}$ of 20 is ▢

**2** What fraction of 1 litre is in each container?

a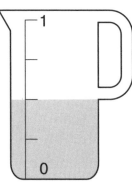

▢

b

▢

c

▢

d

▢

**3** Answer these.

| a    What fraction of £1 is: | b    What fraction of £2 is: | c    What fraction of £10 is: |
|---|---|---|
| 50p ⟶ $\frac{1}{2}$ | 20p ⟶ ☐ | £2.50 ⟶ ☐ |
| 20p ⟶ ☐ | 10p ⟶ ☐ | £5 ⟶ ☐ |
| 10p ⟶ ☐ | 50p ⟶ ☐ | £1 ⟶ ☐ |
| 25p ⟶ ☐ | £1 ⟶ ☐ | £2 ⟶ ☐ |

**4** Answer these.

**a**    An oil drum holds 35 litres, $\frac{1}{5}$ of the oil is poured into bottles.

How much oil is poured into bottles? ☐ litres

**b**    How many minutes are there in $\frac{1}{10}$ of one hour? ☐ minutes

**c**    A necklace has 32 beads, $\frac{1}{8}$ of the beads are red. How many beads are red? ☐ beads

**d**    A roll of cloth is 24 metres long. Sam buys $\frac{3}{4}$ of the roll.

What is the length of the cloth he buys? ☐ metres

**e**    There are 35 bananas on a market stall. Donna buys $\frac{1}{5}$ of the bananas.

How many does she buy? ☐ bananas

**f**    James has £48. He spends $\frac{1}{4}$ of his money on a new coat. How much does the coat cost? £ ☐

**g**    Would it be lighter to carry $\frac{1}{5}$ of 10 kg or $\frac{1}{10}$ of 10 kg? ☐

**h**    There are 24 hours in a day. Robert spends a quarter of the day at school and a third of the day asleep.

Does he spend more time at school or more time sleeping? ☐

**5** Marvin has a box of stickers. He shares them between 3 people and has 1 left over.

He shares them between 4 people and still has 1 left over.

He knows he has fewer than 20 stickers.

How many stickers has he got? [ ]

**6** An ice-cream shop sells 3 different sized cones and 4 different flavours.

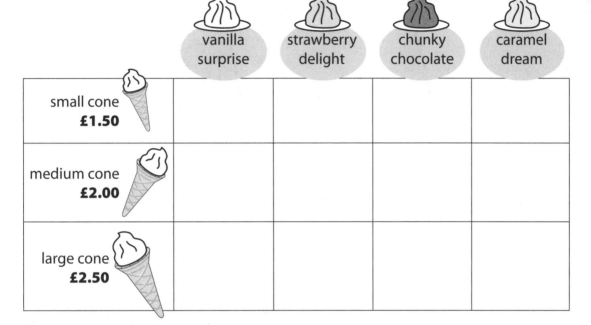

|  | vanilla surprise | strawberry delight | chunky chocolate | caramel dream |
|---|---|---|---|---|
| small cone £1.50 |  |  |  |  |
| medium cone £2.00 |  |  |  |  |
| large cone £2.50 |  |  |  |  |

**a** How many different types of ice-creams can you make? [ ]

**b** Complete this to show the total costs for a family.

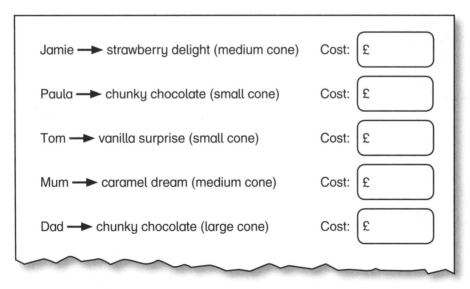

Jamie → strawberry delight (medium cone)    Cost: £ [ ]

Paula → chunky chocolate (small cone)    Cost: £ [ ]

Tom → vanilla surprise (small cone)    Cost: £ [ ]

Mum → caramel dream (medium cone)    Cost: £ [ ]

Dad → chunky chocolate (large cone)    Cost: £ [ ]

Total cost: £ [ ]

# Unit 4 Angles and shapes

 **1** Join each shape to its matching name.

Cube

Cuboid

Cylinder

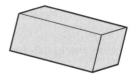

Sphere

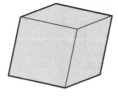

Pyramid

Cone

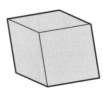

## 2

Name the shapes in each set. Then find the odd one out.
Complete each sentence.

**a**

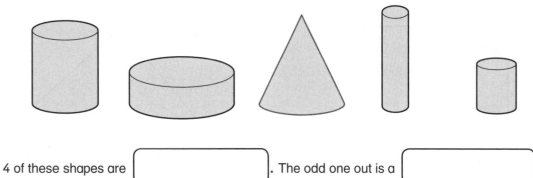

4 of these shapes are [ ]. The odd one out is a [ ].

**b**

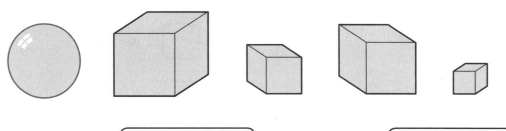

4 of these shapes are [ ]. The odd one out is a [ ].

**c**

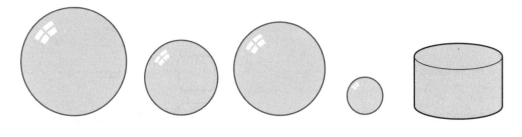

4 of these shapes are [ ]. The odd one out is a [ ].

**d**

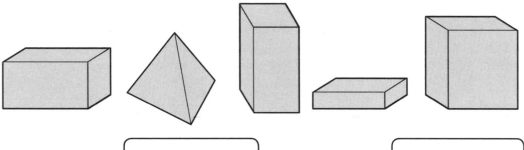

4 of these shapes are [ ]. The odd one out is a [ ].

**3** Write the missing number of faces, edges, surfaces and vertices for each shape.

**a**

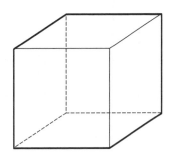

☐ square faces

8 vertices

**c**

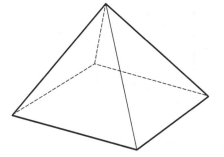

1 square face

☐ triangle faces

☐ vertices

**b**

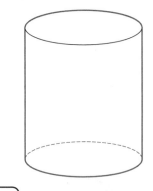

☐ circle faces

1 curved surface

☐ curved edges

**d**

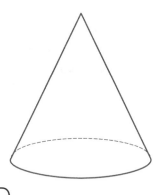

☐ circle face

☐ curved surface

☐ curved edge

**4** Look at these shapes. Write the correct shape letters to answer these.

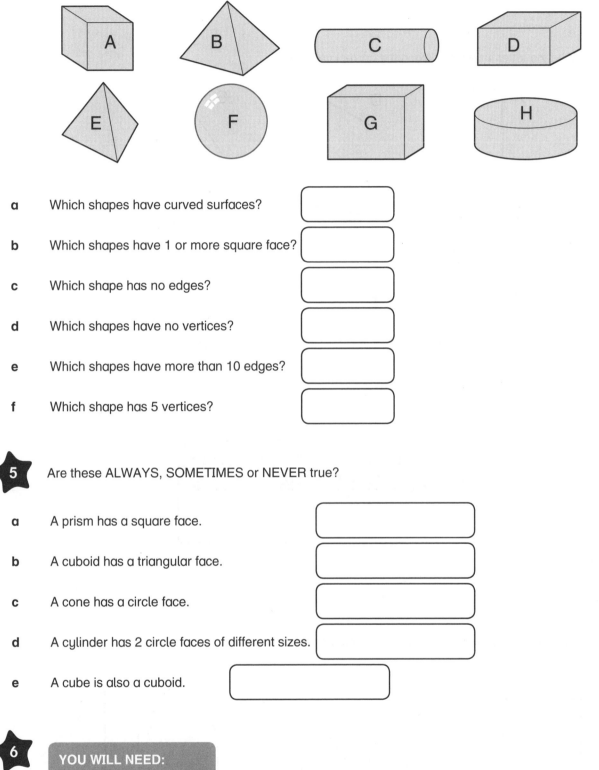

a   Which shapes have curved surfaces?

b   Which shapes have 1 or more square face?

c   Which shape has no edges?

d   Which shapes have no vertices?

e   Which shapes have more than 10 edges?

f   Which shape has 5 vertices?

**5** Are these ALWAYS, SOMETIMES or NEVER true?

a   A prism has a square face.

b   A cuboid has a triangular face.

c   A cone has a circle face.

d   A cylinder has 2 circle faces of different sizes.

e   A cube is also a cuboid.

**6**

YOU WILL NEED:
• **straws**
• **sticky tape**

Make a model using straws and tape of a shape with 5 faces, 8 edges and 5 vertices.

What is the name of your shape?

**1** Write the letter for each angle in the correct column.

A

D

G

B
E

H

C

F

I
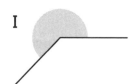

| Right angle | Less than a right angle | Greater than a right angle |
|---|---|---|
|  |  |  |

**2** Draw small squares to show the right angles on each shape.

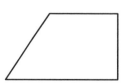

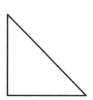

**3** For each shape write the number of each type of angle.

| Shape | Number of right angles | Number of angles less than right angle | Number of angles greater than right angle |
|---|---|---|---|
| a | | | |
| b | | | |
| c | | | |
| d | | | |
| e | | | |
| f | | | |

**4** Cut out 4 different length strips of card and 4 strips of the same length.

Put them together to make different shapes with 4 sides.

Explore the different angles you can make by joining 4 strips.

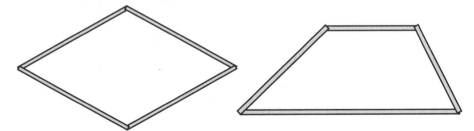

How many right angles can you make in a shape?

How many angles can you make that are smaller than a right angle?

How many angles can you make that are greater than a right angle?

Now explore shapes with 5 sides and 5 angles.

# Number and place value

**1**   Look at this 100 square.

| 1 | 2 | 3 | 4 | 5 | 6 | 7 | 8 | 9 | 10 |
|---|---|---|---|---|---|---|---|---|---|
| 11 | 12 | 13 | 14 | 15 | 16 | 17 | 18 | 19 | 20 |
| 21 | 22 | 23 | 24 | 25 | 26 | 27 | 28 | 29 | 30 |
| 31 | 32 | 33 | 34 | 35 | 36 | 37 | 38 | 39 | 40 |
| 41 | 42 | 43 | 44 | 45 | 46 | 47 | 48 | 49 | 50 |
| 51 | 52 | 53 | 54 | 55 | 56 | 57 | 58 | 59 | 60 |
| 61 | 62 | 63 | 64 | 65 | 66 | 67 | 68 | 69 | 70 |
| 71 | 72 | 73 | 74 | 75 | 76 | 77 | 78 | 79 | 80 |
| 81 | 82 | 83 | 84 | 85 | 86 | 87 | 88 | 89 | 90 |
| 91 | 92 | 93 | 94 | 95 | 96 | 97 | 98 | 99 | 100 |

Start at 4 and count on in 4s. Colour each number.

Now count on in 8s from 8. Cross out these numbers.

What do you notice?

**2**   Write the missing numbers in each sequence.

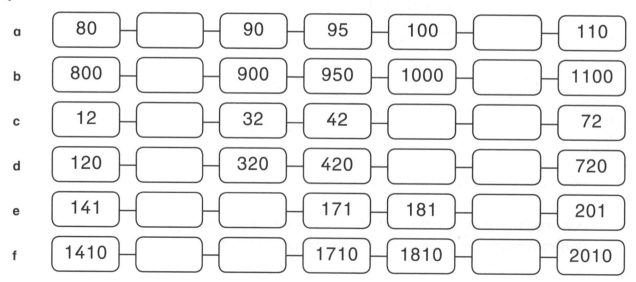

a   80 — ⬜ — 90 — 95 — 100 — ⬜ — 110

b   800 — ⬜ — 900 — 950 — 1000 — ⬜ — 1100

c   12 — ⬜ — 32 — 42 — ⬜ — ⬜ — 72

d   120 — ⬜ — 320 — 420 — ⬜ — ⬜ — 720

e   141 — ⬜ — ⬜ — 171 — 181 — ⬜ — 201

f   1410 — ⬜ — ⬜ — 1710 — 1810 — ⬜ — 2010

**3** Look at each abacus. Complete the sentences.

**a**

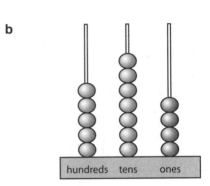

10 more than 415 is ☐

10 less than 415 is ☐

100 more than 415 is ☐

100 less than 415 is ☐

**b**

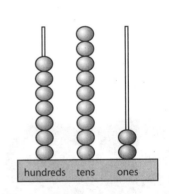

10 more than 574 is ☐

10 less than 574 is ☐

100 more than 574 is ☐

100 less than 574 is ☐

**c**

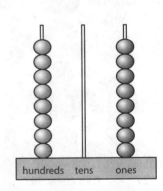

10 more than 792 is ☐

10 less than 792 is ☐

100 more than 792 is ☐

100 less than 792 is ☐

**d**

10 more than 808 is ☐

10 less than 808 is ☐

100 more than 808 is ☐

100 less than 808 is ☐

**4** Count in these steps. Write the missing numbers.

| | | | | | | |
|---|---|---|---|---|---|---|
| a | Count in 10s → | 72 | ☐ | ☐ | ☐ | 112 |
| b | Count in 10s → | 372 | ☐ | ☐ | ☐ | 412 |
| c | Count in 5s → | 72 | ☐ | ☐ | ☐ | 92 |
| d | Count in 5s → | 372 | ☐ | ☐ | ☐ | 392 |
| e | Count in 100s → | 59 | ☐ | ☐ | ☐ | 459 |
| f | Count in 100s → | 61 | ☐ | ☐ | ☐ | 461 |
| g | Count in 50s → | 59 | ☐ | ☐ | ☐ | 259 |
| h | Count in 50s → | 61 | ☐ | ☐ | ☐ | 261 |

**5** Start at each spaceship and follow the sequence to find its planet.
Draw a line to show each path across the stars.

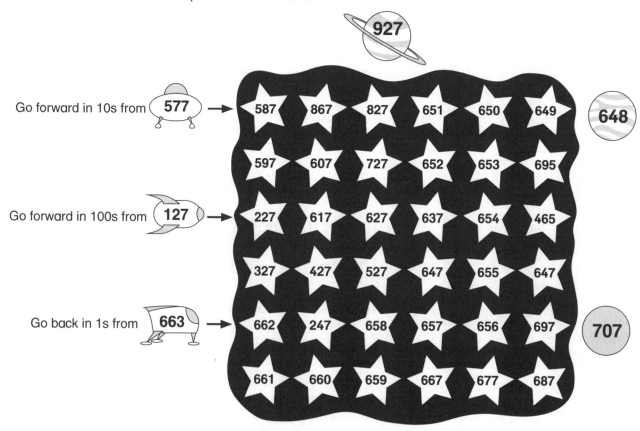

**6** This pictogram shows the number of books sold each day for a week.

| | |
|---|---|
| **Monday** | 🐱🐱🐱🐱 |
| **Tuesday** | 🐱🐱🐱🐱🐱🐱🐱 |
| **Wednesday** | 🐱🐱🐱🐱🐱🐱🐱🐱🐱🐱🐱 |
| **Thursday** | 🐱🐱🐱🐱🐱🐱🐱🐱🐱 |
| **Friday** | 🐱🐱🐱🐱🐱 |
| **Saturday** | 🐱🐱🐱🐱 |
| **Sunday** | 🐱🐱🐱🐱🐱🐱 |

🐱 = 5

**a** How many books were sold in total on Thursday? ☐ books

**b** On which day were 45 books sold? ☐

**c** How many more books were sold on Wednesday than on Monday? ☐ books

**d** How many books were sold altogether on Saturday and Sunday? ☐ books

**1** Write the numbers shown by the Base 10 apparatus.

**a**

| Hundreds | Tens | Ones |
|---|---|---|

[ ] hundreds [ ] tens [ ] ones → [ ]

**b**

| Hundreds | Tens | Ones |
|---|---|---|

[ ] hundreds [ ] tens [ ] ones → [ ]

**c**

| Hundreds | Tens | Ones |
|---|---|---|

[ ] hundreds [ ] tens [ ] ones → [ ]

**d**

| Hundreds | Tens | Ones |
|---|---|---|

[ ] hundreds [ ] tens [ ] ones → [ ]

**e**

| Hundreds | Tens | Ones |
|---|---|---|
| 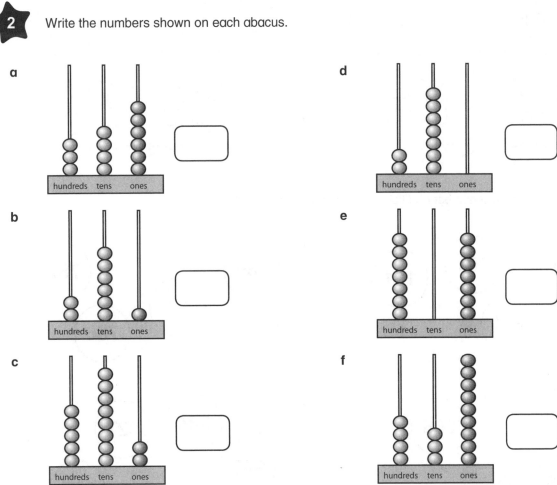 | | |

⬡ hundreds ⬡ tens ⬡ ones ➡ ⬡

**f**

| Hundreds | Tens | Ones |
|---|---|---|
| | | |

⬡ hundreds ⬡ tens ⬡ ones ➡ ⬡

**2** Write the numbers shown on each abacus.

**a**

hundreds   tens   ones

**b**

hundreds   tens   ones

**c**

hundreds   tens   ones

**d**

hundreds   tens   ones

**e**

hundreds   tens   ones

**f**

hundreds   tens   ones

Compare your answers for questions 1 and 2.

**3** Circle the digit in each number that shows these values.

**a** Which digit shows 100?        **1     1     1**

**b** Which digit shows 30?        **3     3     3**

**c** Which digit shows 4?        **4     4     4**

**d** Which digit shows 90?        **9     9     9**

**e** Which digit shows 500?        **5     5     5**

 **4** Write the missing < or > sign for each pair of numbers.

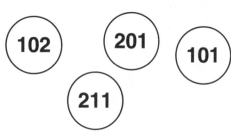

**a** 302   203        **d** 675   576

**b** 589   598        **e** 315   350

**c** 472   471        **f** 922   933

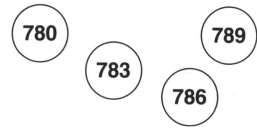

 **5** Circle the smallest number and tick the largest number in each group.

**a** 102   201   101   211

**c** 780   783   789   786

**b** 556   566   555   565

**d** 934   927   947   973

**6** Write each set of prices in order, starting with the lowest price.

£395    £410
£359

£359 < £395 < £410

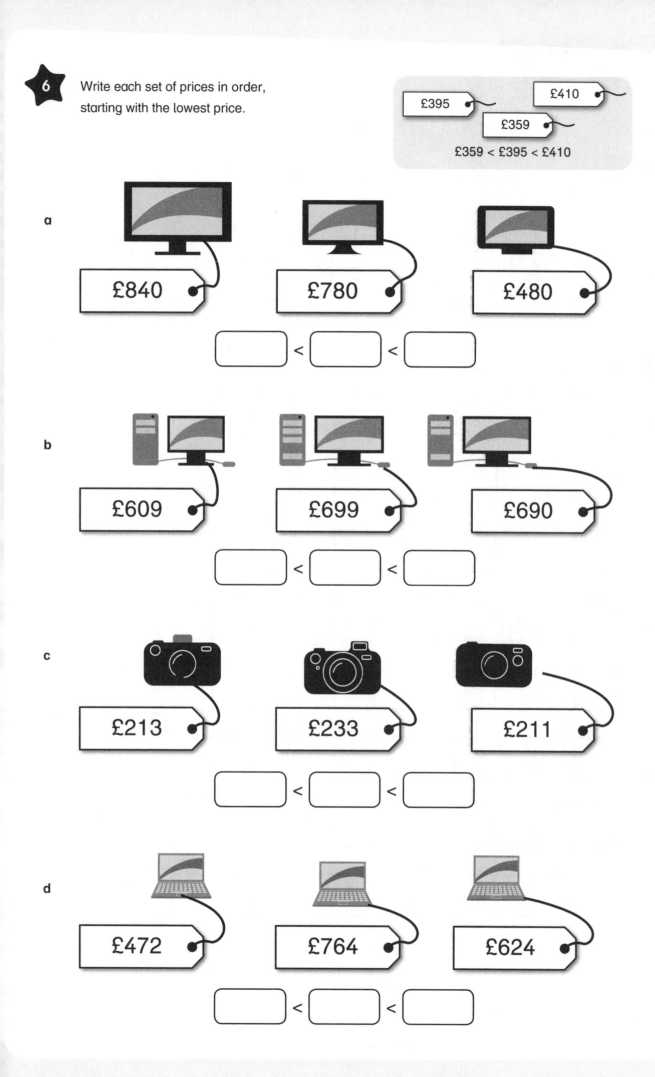

a

£840    £780    £480

[ ] < [ ] < [ ]

b

£609    £699    £690

[ ] < [ ] < [ ]

c

£213    £233    £211

[ ] < [ ] < [ ]

d

£472    £764    £624

[ ] < [ ] < [ ]

**1** Write the tenths value for each position on this number line.

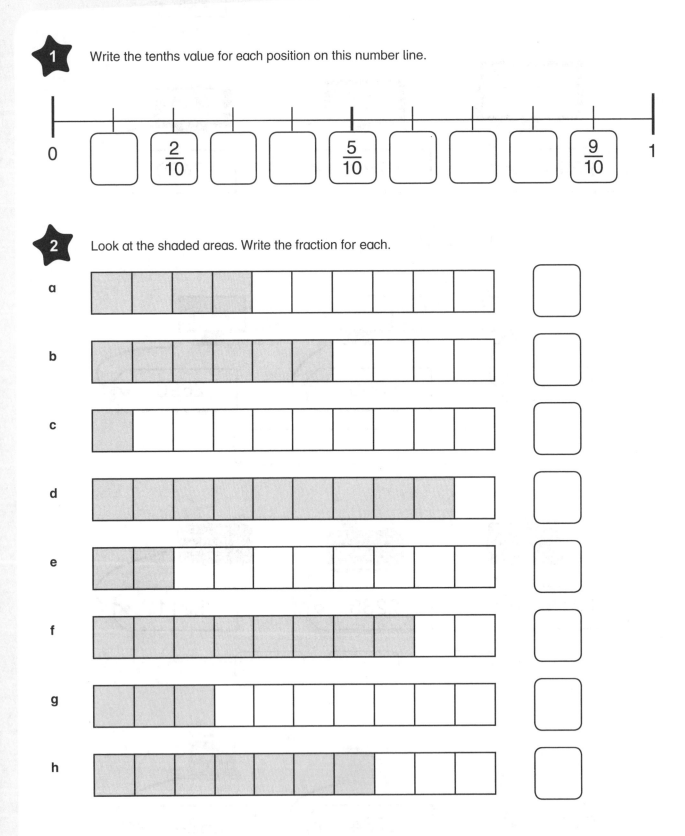

0 ⬜ $\frac{2}{10}$ ⬜ ⬜ $\frac{5}{10}$ ⬜ ⬜ ⬜ $\frac{9}{10}$ 1

**2** Look at the shaded areas. Write the fraction for each.

a ⬜

b ⬜

c ⬜

d ⬜

e ⬜

f ⬜

g ⬜

h ⬜

**3** Complete these.

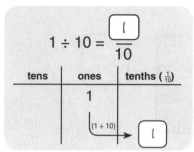

$1 \div 10 = \dfrac{\boxed{1}}{10}$

| tens | ones | tenths ($\frac{1}{10}$) |
|------|------|------|
|  | 1 |  |

(1 ÷ 10) → $\boxed{1}$

**a**

$2 \div 10 = \dfrac{\boxed{\phantom{0}}}{10}$

| tens | ones | tenths ($\frac{1}{10}$) |
|------|------|------|
|  | 2 |  |

(2 ÷ 10) → $\boxed{\phantom{0}}$

**b**

$3 \div 10 = \dfrac{\boxed{\phantom{0}}}{10}$

| tens | ones | tenths ($\frac{1}{10}$) |
|------|------|------|
|  | 3 |  |

(3 ÷ 10) → $\boxed{\phantom{0}}$

**c**

$4 \div 10 = \dfrac{\boxed{\phantom{0}}}{10}$

| tens | ones | tenths ($\frac{1}{10}$) |
|------|------|------|
|  | 4 |  |

(4 ÷ 10) → $\boxed{\phantom{0}}$

**d**

$5 \div 10 = \dfrac{\boxed{\phantom{0}}}{10}$

| tens | ones | tenths ($\frac{1}{10}$) |
|------|------|------|
|  | 5 |  |

(5 ÷ 10) → $\boxed{\phantom{0}}$

**e**

$6 \div 10 = \dfrac{\boxed{\phantom{0}}}{10}$

| tens | ones | tenths ($\frac{1}{10}$) |
|------|------|------|
|  | 6 |  |

(6 ÷ 10) → $\boxed{\phantom{0}}$

**f**

$7 \div 10 = \dfrac{\boxed{\phantom{0}}}{10}$

| tens | ones | tenths ($\frac{1}{10}$) |
|------|------|------|
|  | 7 |  |

(7 ÷ 10) → $\boxed{\phantom{0}}$

**g**

$8 \div 10 = \dfrac{\boxed{\phantom{0}}}{10}$

| tens | ones | tenths ($\frac{1}{10}$) |
|------|------|------|
|  | 8 |  |

(8 ÷ 10) → $\boxed{\phantom{0}}$

**h**

$9 \div 10 = \dfrac{\boxed{\phantom{0}}}{10}$

| tens | ones | tenths ($\frac{1}{10}$) |
|------|------|------|
|  | 9 |  |

(9 ÷ 10) → $\boxed{\phantom{0}}$

**i**

$10 \div 10 = \dfrac{\boxed{\phantom{0}}}{10}$

| tens | ones | tenths ($\frac{1}{10}$) |
|------|------|------|
| 1 | 0 |  |

(10 ÷ 10) → $\boxed{\phantom{0}}$

**4** Tick the pictures that show tenths.

☐

☐

☐

☐

☐

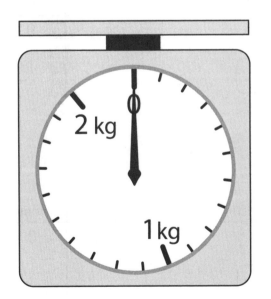

☐

# Unit 6 — Addition and subtraction

## 6a Adding 3-digit numbers

 **1** Answer these.

**a**

4 + 8 =

40 + 80 =

46 + 80 =

400 + 800 =

460 + 800 =

**b**

7 + 6 =

70 + 60 =

73 + 60 =

700 + 600 =

730 + 600 =

**c**

9 + 5 =

90 + 50 =

95 + 50 =

900 + 500 =

950 + 500 =

 **2** The 3 outside numbers total the centre number.
Write the missing numbers.

**a**
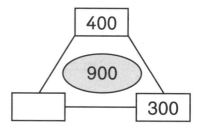

**c**
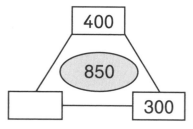

**b**
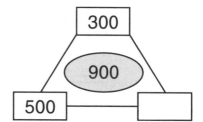

**d**
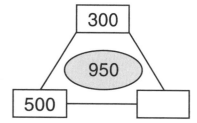

53

**3** This chart shows the points scored by 4 players for 2 rounds of a computer game.
What are their total scores?

| Player | Round 1 | Round 2 | Total |
|--------|---------|---------|-------|
| Alec | 233 points | 60 points | |
| Ben | 140 points | 130 points | |
| Claire | 382 points | 200 points | |
| Deena | 210 points | 190 points | |

 **4** Answer these.

**a**
```
   1  5  4
+  6  3  1
```

**d**
```
   4  7  0
+  3  4  3
```

**g**
```
   5  4  6
+  7  3  5
```

**b**
```
   7  0  3
+  2  9  5
```

**e**
```
   3  1  2
+  4  8  9
```

**h**
```
   8  8  4
+  3  1  9
```

**c**
```
   3  2  5
+  5  4  9
```

**f**
```
   3  9  5
+  8  0  6
```

**i**
```
   6  5  8
+  7  5  9
```

**5** Answer these.

**a** A tennis racket costs £138. How much do 2 tennis rackets cost? £ _____

**b** There are 249 children in Rob's school and 193 children in Zoe's school. How many children are there in total in the 2 schools? _____ children

**c** A lorry travels 156 km to collect boxes of vegetables from a farm and 147 km back to the market in the town. How far does the lorry travel in total? _____ km

**d** A table cost £670 and a set of chairs cost £97. How much is this in total? £ _____

**e** Jim buys a suit for £196 and a coat for £115. How much does he spend altogether? £ _____

**f** A car has enough petrol for 300 km. The driver will need to travel 79 km to collect a passenger from the airport and another 145 km to take the passenger to a town. The driver will then need to drive 68 km back home. Will he have enough petrol for the whole journey? _____

**6** Complete these, writing in the digits 1, 2, 3, 4, 5 and 6.

$$
\begin{array}{r}
6\ \square\ 7 \\
+\ \square\ 1\ 9 \\
\hline
8\ 6\ \square
\end{array}
\qquad
\begin{array}{r}
7\ 9\ \square \\
+\ \square\ 5\ 9 \\
\hline
9\ \square\ 2
\end{array}
$$

**1** Answer these.

a   900 – 700 = [ ]        924 – [ ] = 224

b   800 – 600 = [ ]        824 – [ ] = 224

c   700 – 500 = [ ]        724 – [ ] = 224

d   600 – 400 = [ ]        624 – [ ] = 224

e   500 – 300 = [ ]        524 – [ ] = 224

f   400 – 200 = [ ]        424 – [ ] = 224

 **2** Write the 4 number facts this bar model shows.

| 648 | |
|---|---|
| 319 | 329 |

[ ] + [ ] = [ ]

[ ] + [ ] = [ ]

[ ] – [ ] = [ ]

[ ] – [ ] = [ ]

 **3**

**YOU WILL NEED:**
• **Base 10 apparatus**

Complete these. Use Base 10 apparatus to help.

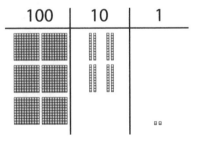

a
```
    5 7 6
  – 1 3 5
  ─────────
```
[ ]

```
    7 6 4
  – 2 3 1
  ─────────
```
[ ]

```
    9 6 5
  – 4 1 4
  ─────────
```
[ ]

56

**b**

| | 5 | 7 | 6 |
|---|---|---|---|
| − | 1 | 3 | 7 |

| | 7 | 6 | 4 |
|---|---|---|---|
| − | 2 | 3 | 8 |

| | 9 | 6 | 5 |
|---|---|---|---|
| − | 4 | 1 | 8 |

**c**

| | 5 | 7 | 6 |
|---|---|---|---|
| − | 1 | 8 | 5 |

| | 7 | 6 | 4 |
|---|---|---|---|
| − | 2 | 8 | 1 |

| | 9 | 6 | 5 |
|---|---|---|---|
| − | 5 | 9 | 4 |

**d**

| | 5 | 7 | 6 |
|---|---|---|---|
| − | 1 | 8 | 7 |

| | 7 | 6 | 4 |
|---|---|---|---|
| − | 2 | 7 | 8 |

| | 9 | 6 | 5 |
|---|---|---|---|
| − | 7 | 9 | 8 |

What is the same and what is different about each row?

⭐ **4** What is the difference between these pairs of numbers?
Count on the number line to show your method.

**a**

341        584

Difference is ☐

**b**

235        608

Difference is ☐

**c**

392        481

Difference is ☐

**d**

457        793

Difference is ☐

**5** Look at the heights of the Jones family. Answer these questions.

183 cm

157 cm

138 cm

119 cm

**Sam**     **Becky**

**a** How much taller is Mr Jones than Mrs Jones? [ ] cm

**b** How much shorter is Becky than her mother? [ ] cm

**c** If Sam grows up to be the same height as his father how many more centimetres will he need to grow? [ ] cm

**d** What is the difference in height between Sam and Becky? [ ] cm

**6** The digits 1, 2, 3 and 4 are missing from these. Complete them.

```
    6  9  ☐              7  ☐  8
 -  ☐  8  1           -  6  1  5
   ─────────            ─────────
    4  1  3              1  3  ☐
   ─────────            ─────────
```

# Writing and using fractions

 **1** Draw beads on each abacus to show these numbers.

**a**

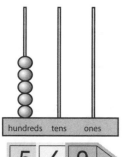

hundreds tens ones

5 4 9

**d**

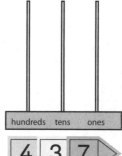

hundreds tens ones

4 3 7

**b**

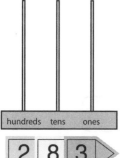

hundreds tens ones

2 8 3

**e**

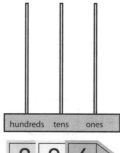

hundreds tens ones

3 9 4

**c**

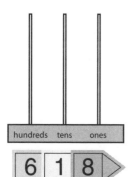

hundreds tens ones

6 1 8

**f**

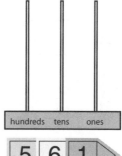

hundreds tens ones

5 6 1

2 Write the numbers shown for each of these.

**a**

[ ] hundreds [ ] tens [ ] ones → [ ]

**b**

[ ] hundreds [ ] tens [ ] ones → [ ]

**c**

[ ] hundreds [ ] tens [ ] ones → [ ]

**d**

[ ] hundreds [ ] tens [ ] ones → [ ]

**e**

[ ] hundreds [ ] tens [ ] ones → [ ]

**f**

[ ] hundreds [ ] tens [ ] ones → [ ]

Now compare the numbers and pictures in questions 1 and 2.

**3** What are the numbers shown on these place-value grids?

**a**

| 100s | 10s | 1s |
|---|---|---|
| ○ ○ | ○ ○ ○ ○ ○ | ○ ○ ○ |

☐

**c**

| 100s | 10s | 1s |
|---|---|---|
| ○ ○ ○ | ○ ○ ○ ○ ○ | ○ ○ |

☐

**b**

| 100s | 10s | 1s |
|---|---|---|
| ○ ○ ○ ○ ○ | ○ ○ ○ | ○ ○ |

☐

**d**

| 100s | 10s | 1s |
|---|---|---|
| ○ ○ | ○ ○ ○ | ○ ○ ○ ○ ○ |

☐

**4**

| YOU WILL NEED: |
|---|
| • **10 counters** |

Use 10 counters on this place-value grid.

| 100s | 10s | 1s |
|---|---|---|
|  |  |  |

**a** What is the largest number you can make? ☐

**b** What is the smallest number you can make? ☐

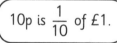

10p is $\frac{1}{10}$ of £1.

**5** Complete these.

**a** 10p + 10p = ☐ p          $\frac{1}{10} + \frac{1}{10} = \frac{\square}{10}$

**b** 10p + 20p = ☐ p          $\frac{1}{10} + \frac{2}{10} = \frac{\square}{10}$

**c** 20p + 20p = ☐ p          $\frac{2}{10} + \frac{2}{10} = \frac{\square}{10}$

**d** 20p + 30p = ☐ p          $\frac{2}{10} + \frac{3}{10} = \frac{\square}{10}$

**e** 30p + 30p = ☐ p          $\frac{3}{10} + \frac{3}{10} = \frac{\square}{10}$

**1** Look at the fractions shaded in each shape.

Draw a line to join each shape to the matching fraction and fraction word.

$\frac{1}{4}$  one-sixth

$\frac{1}{2}$  one-third

$\frac{1}{3}$  one-quarter

$\frac{1}{6}$ 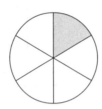 one-half

$\frac{1}{5}$  one-fifth

 Write the fractions shown on each fraction bar.

a $\frac{2}{\boxed{\phantom{0}}}$

b $\frac{3}{\boxed{\phantom{0}}}$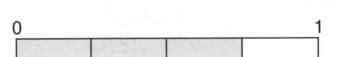

c $\frac{3}{\boxed{\phantom{0}}}$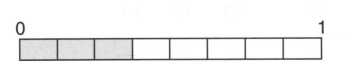

**d**  $\dfrac{2}{\boxed{\phantom{0}}}$

**e**  $\dfrac{6}{\boxed{\phantom{0}}}$

**f**  $\dfrac{4}{\boxed{\phantom{0}}}$

**3** Write the fraction shown by each arrow on these number lines.

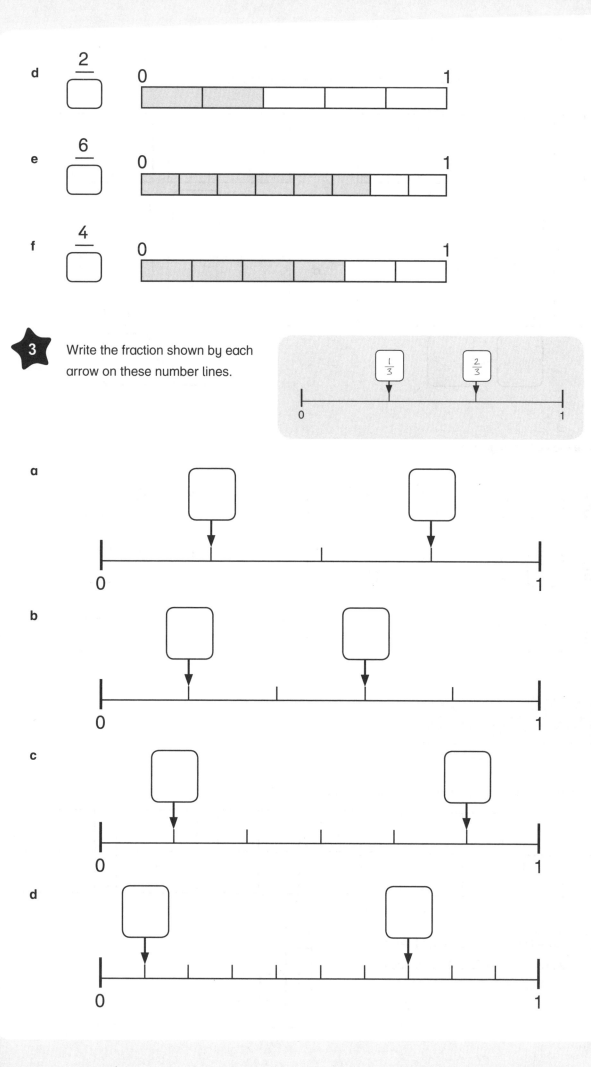

**a**

**b**

**c**

**d**

**4** Write the fractions for each pair of shapes to make the sentence true.

**a**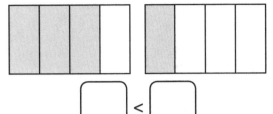

$\boxed{\phantom{0}}$ < $\boxed{\phantom{0}}$

**c**

$\boxed{\phantom{0}}$ > $\boxed{\phantom{0}}$

**b**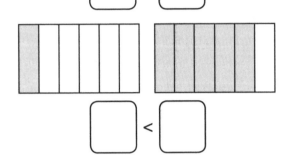

$\boxed{\phantom{0}}$ < $\boxed{\phantom{0}}$

**d**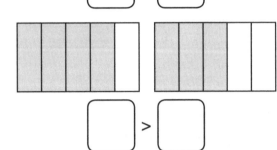

$\boxed{\phantom{0}}$ > $\boxed{\phantom{0}}$

 **5** Write the correct sign < or >

**a** $\dfrac{1}{5}$ $\bigcirc$ $\dfrac{3}{5}$

**d** $\dfrac{4}{5}$ $\bigcirc$ $\dfrac{2}{5}$

**g** $\dfrac{9}{10}$ $\bigcirc$ $\dfrac{3}{10}$

**b** $\dfrac{5}{6}$ $\bigcirc$ $\dfrac{1}{6}$

**e** $\dfrac{3}{10}$ $\bigcirc$ $\dfrac{7}{10}$

**h** $\dfrac{7}{12}$ $\bigcirc$ $\dfrac{11}{12}$

**c** $\dfrac{1}{3}$ $\bigcirc$ $\dfrac{2}{3}$

**f** $\dfrac{5}{8}$ $\bigcirc$ $\dfrac{7}{8}$

**i** $\dfrac{3}{5}$ $\bigcirc$ $\dfrac{2}{5}$

 **6**

**YOU WILL NEED:**
- **coloured pencils**
- **squared paper**

**a** How many different ways can you colour $\frac{1}{2}$ of these grids?

     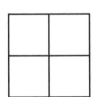

**b** Use squared paper to draw a grid like this. Explore how many different ways you can colour $\frac{1}{2}$ of this grid.

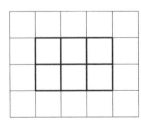

**1** Join pairs of fractions that total 1.

$\frac{1}{6}$    $\frac{1}{5}$    $\frac{3}{5}$    $\frac{5}{6}$

$\frac{1}{4}$    $\frac{4}{5}$    $\frac{2}{5}$    $\frac{3}{4}$

$\frac{2}{6}$    $\frac{4}{6}$

**2** Add these fractions. Colour the fraction bar to show the addition.

> **YOU WILL NEED:**
> • coloured pencils

**a**   $\frac{1}{3} + \frac{1}{3} = \boxed{\phantom{0}}$

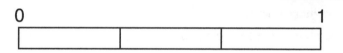

**b**   $\frac{1}{4} + \frac{1}{4} = \boxed{\phantom{0}}$

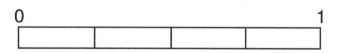

**c**   $\frac{1}{5} + \frac{1}{5} = \boxed{\phantom{0}}$

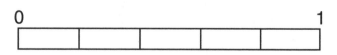

**d**   $\frac{1}{6} + \frac{1}{6} = \boxed{\phantom{0}}$

**3** Add these fractions.

**a** $\dfrac{1}{5} + \dfrac{3}{5} = \boxed{\phantom{0}}$

**b** $\dfrac{3}{10} + \dfrac{4}{10} = \boxed{\phantom{0}}$

**c** $\dfrac{3}{8} + \dfrac{2}{8} = \boxed{\phantom{0}}$

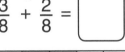

**d** $\dfrac{2}{6} + \dfrac{3}{6} = \boxed{\phantom{0}}$

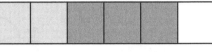

**e** $\dfrac{1}{8} + \dfrac{5}{8} = \boxed{\phantom{0}}$

**f** $\dfrac{1}{5} + \dfrac{3}{5} = \boxed{\phantom{0}}$

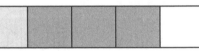

 **4**

$\dfrac{3}{5} - \dfrac{1}{5} = \boxed{\dfrac{2}{5}}$

Subtract these fractions.

Use the number lines to help you.

**a** $\dfrac{2}{3} - \dfrac{1}{3} = \boxed{\phantom{0}}$

**b** $\dfrac{3}{5} - \dfrac{2}{5} = \boxed{\phantom{0}}$

**c** $\dfrac{5}{6} - \dfrac{1}{6} = \boxed{\phantom{0}}$

**d** $\dfrac{5}{8} - \dfrac{1}{8} = \boxed{\phantom{0}}$

**5** Subtract these fractions. Cross out
fractions of each rectangle to help you.

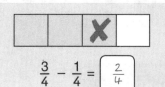

$$\frac{3}{4} - \frac{1}{4} = \boxed{\frac{2}{4}}$$

**a**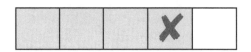

$$\frac{4}{5} - \frac{1}{5} = \boxed{\phantom{0}}$$

**d**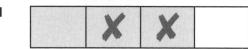

$$\frac{3}{4} - \frac{2}{4} = \boxed{\phantom{0}}$$

**b**

$$\frac{4}{6} - \frac{2}{6} = \boxed{\phantom{0}}$$

**e**

$$\frac{7}{10} - \frac{5}{10} = \boxed{\phantom{0}}$$

**c**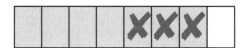

$$\frac{7}{8} - \frac{3}{8} = \boxed{\phantom{0}}$$

**f**

$$\frac{6}{8} - \frac{2}{8} = \boxed{\phantom{0}}$$

**6** Which of these 2 sums is the longer time?

$$\frac{1}{10} \text{ minute} + \frac{1}{3} \text{ minute} + \frac{1}{6} \text{ minute}$$

$$\frac{1}{4} \text{ minute} + \frac{1}{2} \text{ minute}$$

# Using multiplication and division facts

 **1**   Complete each of these.

**a**

3 × 5 = ☐

5 × 3 = ☐

**c**

2 × 6 = ☐

6 × 2 = ☐

**e**

5 × 4 = ☐

4 × 5 = ☐

**b**

4 × 3 = ☐

3 × 4 = ☐

**d**

3 × 8 = ☐

8 × 3 = ☐

**f**

3 × 6 = ☐

6 × 3 = ☐

 **2**   Write the missing numbers.

**a**

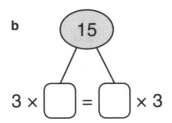

( 12 )

3 × ☐ = ☐ × 3

**c**

( 24 )

4 × ☐ = ☐ × 4

**e**

( 25 )

5 × ☐ = ☐ × 5

**b**

( 15 )

3 × ☐ = ☐ × 3

**d**

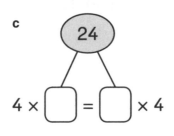

( 28 )

4 × ☐ = ☐ × 4

**f**

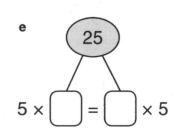

( 30 )

5 × ☐ = ☐ × 5

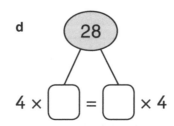
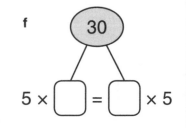

**3** Write the missing numbers.

**a**

Double
6
Halve

**c**

Double
18
Halve

**e**

Double
42
Halve

**b**

Double
6
Halve

**d**
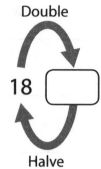
Double
18
Halve

**f**

Double
42
Halve

**4** Continue these doubling chains.

**a**  2  4  8  16  ☐  ☐  ☐

**b**  3  6  12  18  ☐  ☐  ☐

**c**  5  10  20  40  ☐  ☐  ☐

**5** Try to solve this problem.

Jasmin had a letter that cost 42p to post.
She stuck on 9 stamps. Each stamp was worth either 3p or 6p.
How many of each stamp did Jasmin stick on her letter?
Complete this chart to help you solve this problem.

| Number of stamps | 3p stamps | 6p stamps |
|:---:|:---:|:---:|
| 1 | 3p | 6p |
| 2 | | |
| 3 | | |
| 4 | | |
| 5 | | |
| 6 | | |
| 7 | | |
| 8 | | |
| 9 | | |

**6** With a partner, play this multiplying game using the 2 gameboards.

**To play:**

- Each choose your own gameboard.
- Take turns to roll 2 dice (or roll 1 dice twice). Multiply the numbers together.
- Cover a square on your gameboard that matches your answer. If you cannot cover a square, miss that go.
- The winner is the first player to cover 4 squares in a vertical line.

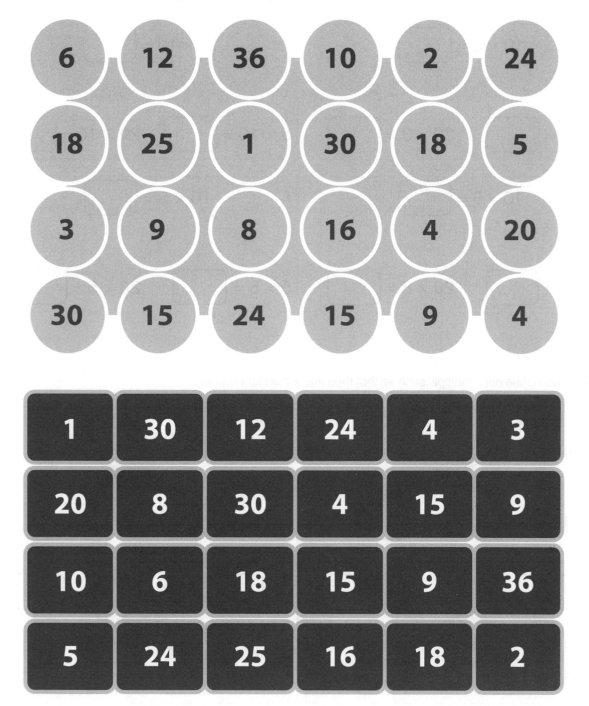

| 6 | 12 | 36 | 10 | 2 | 24 |
| --- | --- | --- | --- | --- | --- |
| 18 | 25 | 1 | 30 | 18 | 5 |
| 3 | 9 | 8 | 16 | 4 | 20 |
| 30 | 15 | 24 | 15 | 9 | 4 |

| 1 | 30 | 12 | 24 | 4 | 3 |
| --- | --- | --- | --- | --- | --- |
| 20 | 8 | 30 | 4 | 15 | 9 |
| 10 | 6 | 18 | 15 | 9 | 36 |
| 5 | 24 | 25 | 16 | 18 | 2 |

**1** Answer these.

**a**
10 × 6 = ☐

5 × 6 = ☐    20 × 6 = ☐

**b**
10 × 3 = ☐

5 × 3 = ☐    20 × 3 = ☐

**c**
10 × 8 = ☐

5 × 8 = ☐    20 × 8 = ☐

**d**
10 × 4 = ☐

5 × 4 = ☐    20 × 4 = ☐

**e**
10 × 10 = ☐

5 × 10 = ☐    20 × 10 = ☐

**f**
10 × 5 = ☐

5 × 5 = ☐    20 × 5 = ☐

**2** Complete each multiplication so that they equal the star number.

**a**
☐ × 10      5 × ☐

20

10 × ☐      ☐ × 5

**b**
☐ × 10      5 × ☐

30

10 × ☐      ☐ × 5

**c**
☐ × 10      5 × ☐

40

10 × ☐      ☐ × 5

**d**
☐ × 10      5 × ☐

60

10 × ☐      ☐ × 5

**3** Complete the facts for each of these.

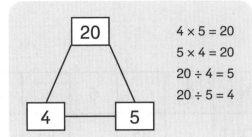

20

$4 \times 5 = 20$
$5 \times 4 = 20$
$20 \div 4 = 5$
$20 \div 5 = 4$

**a**

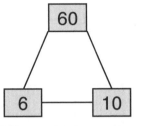

$10 \times \boxed{\phantom{0}} = 60$

$\boxed{\phantom{0}} \times 10 = 60$

$60 \div 10 = \boxed{\phantom{0}}$

$60 \div \boxed{\phantom{0}} = 10$

**c**

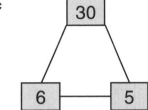

$\boxed{\phantom{0}} \times \boxed{\phantom{0}} = \boxed{\phantom{0}}$

$\boxed{\phantom{0}} \times \boxed{\phantom{0}} = \boxed{\phantom{0}}$

$\boxed{\phantom{0}} \div \boxed{\phantom{0}} = \boxed{\phantom{0}}$

$\boxed{\phantom{0}} \div \boxed{\phantom{0}} = \boxed{\phantom{0}}$

**b**

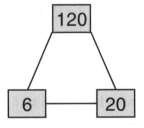

$6 \times \boxed{\phantom{0}} = \boxed{\phantom{0}}$

$\boxed{\phantom{0}} \times 6 = \boxed{\phantom{0}}$

$\boxed{\phantom{0}} \div 6 = \boxed{\phantom{0}}$

$\boxed{\phantom{0}} \div \boxed{\phantom{0}} = 6$

**d**

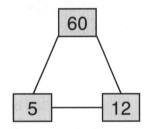

$\boxed{\phantom{0}} \times \boxed{\phantom{0}} = \boxed{\phantom{0}}$

$\boxed{\phantom{0}} \times \boxed{\phantom{0}} = \boxed{\phantom{0}}$

$\boxed{\phantom{0}} \div \boxed{\phantom{0}} = \boxed{\phantom{0}}$

$\boxed{\phantom{0}} \div \boxed{\phantom{0}} = \boxed{\phantom{0}}$

**4** Complete each of these.

a

| IN | 2 | | 5 | | 6 |
|---|---|---|---|---|---|
| OUT | | 35 | | 45 | |

b

| IN | 3 | 8 | | | 5 |
|---|---|---|---|---|---|
| OUT | | | 140 | 80 | |

**5** Write these numbers in the correct place on this Carroll diagram.

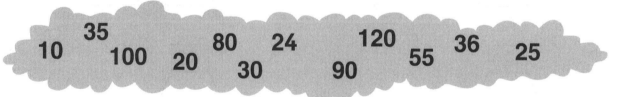

10  35  100  20  80  24  120  55  36  25  30  90

| | Can be divided by 5 | Cannot be divided by 5 |
|---|---|---|
| **Can be divided by 20** | | |
| **Cannot be divided by 20** | | |

74

**1** Complete the facts for each of these.

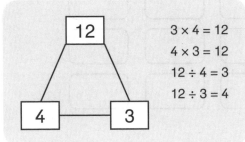

12

3 × 4 = 12
4 × 3 = 12
12 ÷ 4 = 3
12 ÷ 3 = 4

4 — 3

**a**

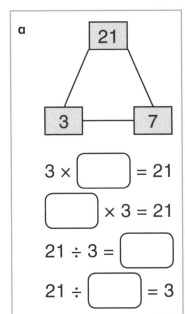

21

3 — 7

3 × ☐ = 21

☐ × 3 = 21

21 ÷ 3 = ☐

21 ÷ ☐ = 3

**c**

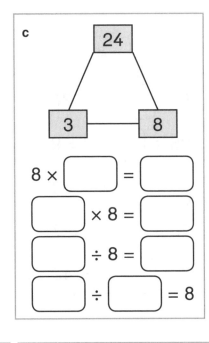

24

3 — 8

8 × ☐ = ☐

☐ × 8 = ☐

☐ ÷ 8 = ☐

☐ ÷ ☐ = 8

**e**

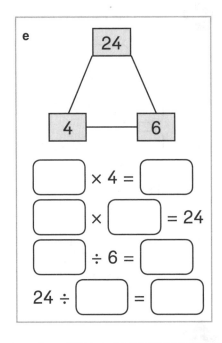

24

4 — 6

☐ × 4 = ☐

☐ × ☐ = 24

☐ ÷ 6 = ☐

24 ÷ ☐ = ☐

**b**

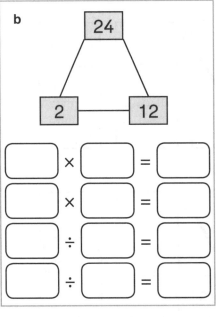

24

2 — 12

☐ × ☐ = ☐

☐ × ☐ = ☐

☐ ÷ ☐ = ☐

☐ ÷ ☐ = ☐

**d**

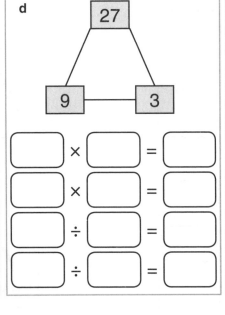

27

9 — 3

☐ × ☐ = ☐

☐ × ☐ = ☐

☐ ÷ ☐ = ☐

☐ ÷ ☐ = ☐

**f**

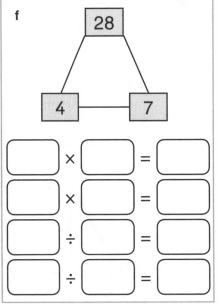

28

4 — 7

☐ × ☐ = ☐

☐ × ☐ = ☐

☐ ÷ ☐ = ☐

☐ ÷ ☐ = ☐

**2** Write 4 possible answers for each missing number.

a 3 ×  > 20

b  × 4 < 20

c 6 ×  > 30

d  × 5 < 30

**3** Write the missing numbers.

a 3 × ⬚ = 15          ⬚ ÷ 6 = 5

b ⬚ ÷ 3 = 6          6 × ⬚ = 36

c ⬚ × 2 = 18          36 ÷ ⬚ = 9

d 16 ÷ ⬚ = 4          ⬚ × 4 = 32

e 7 × ⬚ = 14          28 ÷ ⬚ = 7

f 21 ÷ ⬚ = 7          7 × ⬚ = 42

**4** Write each scaled-up length. They are each 3 times as long.

a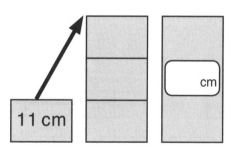

b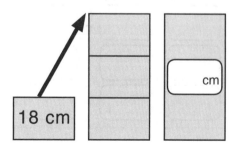

c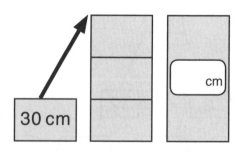

d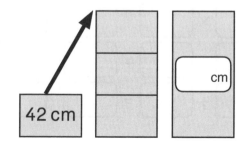

**5** Write each scaled-down length. They are each $\frac{1}{5}$ of the length.

**a**

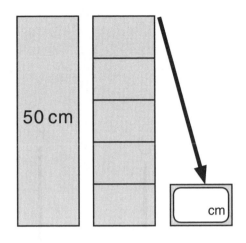

50 cm

☐ cm

**c**

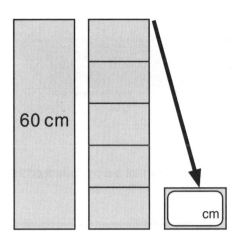

60 cm

☐ cm

**b**

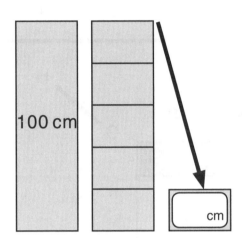

100 cm

☐ cm

**d**

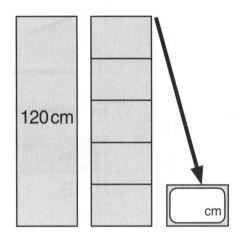

120 cm

☐ cm

**6** What's my number?
Work out the mystery number for each of these.

**a** When I divide my number by 5 the answer is 8.

**b** When I multiply my number by 6 the answer is 42.

**c** When I make my number 4 times as big the answer is 100.

**d** When I make my number $\frac{1}{3}$ of the size the answer is 30.

**e** When I double my number and then add 3 the answer is 17.

**f** When I divide my number by 4 and then subtract 2 the answer is 3.

# Exploring lines and turns

**1** List the lines that are horizontal and those that are vertical.

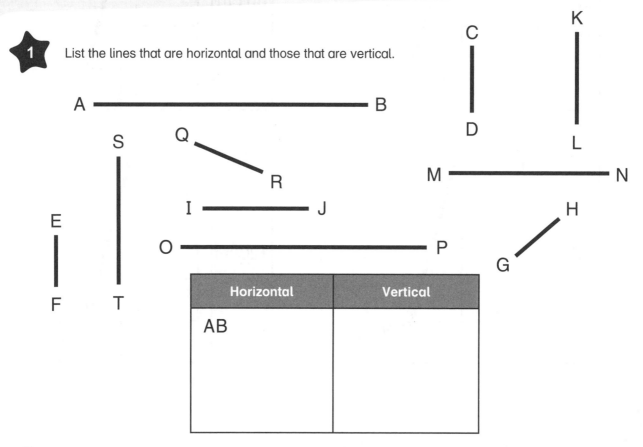

| Horizontal | Vertical |
|------------|----------|
| AB | |

**2** Which of these are parallel lines? Tick the boxes to show them.

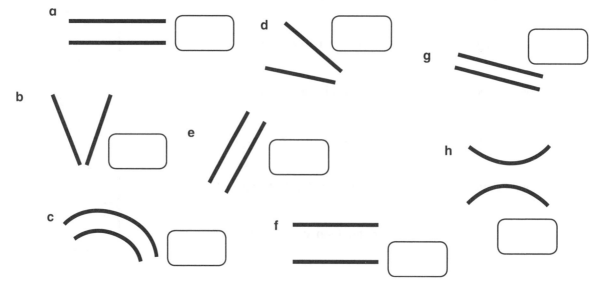

How do you know they are parallel lines?

**3** These are perpendicular lines.

Make a square corner so that you can find and draw perpendicular lines.

- Fold a piece of paper in half.
- Fold it in half again to make a square corner.
- Draw a square on the corner to show the right angle

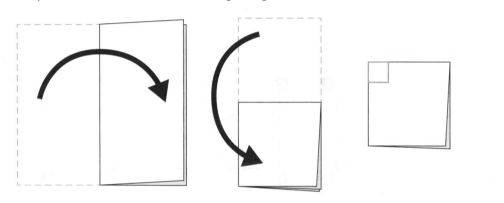

**a** Use your square corner to find items around the room that have perpendicular lines.

**b** Draw a horizontal straight line, 8 cm long in the space below.

Use your square corner and a ruler to draw 3 lines perpendicular to that line.

Make each line a different length.

**c** Are the 3 lines you have drawn parallel to each other?

**4** Which of these are vertical, or perpendicular, to the ground? Write 'vertical' next to the ones that you choose.

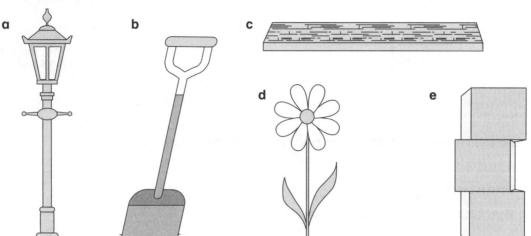

a        b        c

d        e

**5** Look at these shapes.

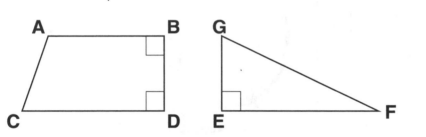
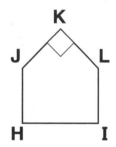

Complete each statement. Use the words perpendicular or parallel.

a   AB is [                    ] to CD       d   AB is [                    ] to BD

b   EF is [                    ] to EG       e   IL is [                    ] to HJ

c   HI is [                    ] to HJ       f   JK is [                    ] to KL

**6** Which of these capital letters has at least 1 pair of parallel lines and 2 perpendicular lines?

# EFHIT

[                    ]

**1** The hour hand makes the following turns. What number does it stop on?

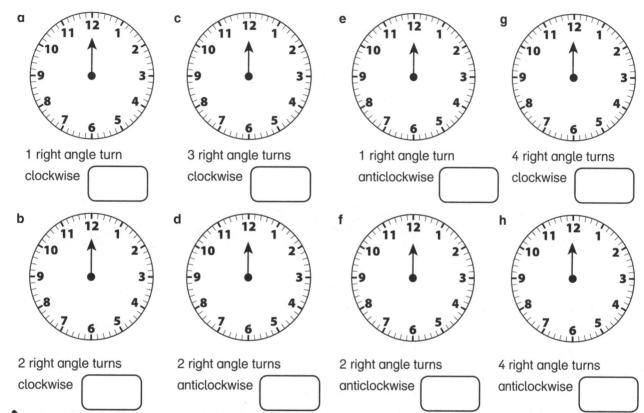

a
1 right angle turn
clockwise

c
3 right angle turns
clockwise

e
1 right angle turn
anticlockwise

g
4 right angle turns
clockwise

b
2 right angle turns
clockwise

d
2 right angle turns
anticlockwise

f
2 right angle turns
anticlockwise

h
4 right angle turns
anticlockwise

**2** The hour hand makes the following turns. Draw the new position of the hour hand.

a

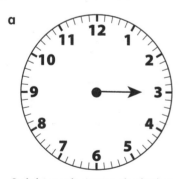

2 right angle turns clockwise

c

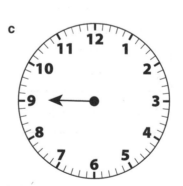

3 right angle turns clockwise

b

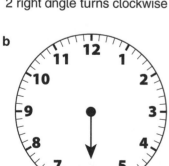

1 right angle turn anticlockwise

d

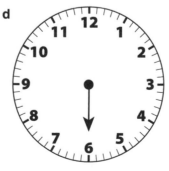

3 right angle turns anticlockwise

This compass shows the 4 compass points.

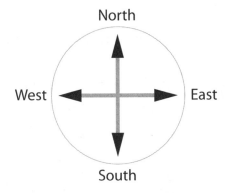

Complete this chart to show the directions you face for each turn.

| Start direction faced | Turn | End direction faced |
|---|---|---|
| North | $\frac{1}{2}$ turn clockwise | |
| North | $\frac{1}{4}$ turn anticlockwise | |
| South | $\frac{3}{4}$ turn clockwise | |
| South | $\frac{1}{4}$ turn anticlockwise | |
| East | $\frac{1}{2}$ turn anticlockwise | |
| East | $\frac{1}{2}$ turn clockwise | |
| West | $\frac{3}{4}$ turn clockwise | |
| West | $\frac{3}{4}$ turn anticlockwise | |

**4**

YOU WILL NEED:
• coloured pencils

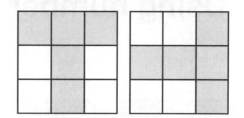

This pattern has made a $\frac{1}{4}$ turn clockwise.

Follow the rules for each turn. Colour the squares to continue the patterns.

**a** $\frac{1}{4}$ turn clockwise

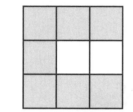 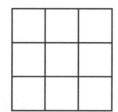 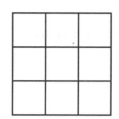 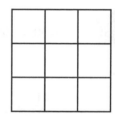

**b** $\frac{1}{2}$ turn clockwise

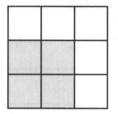 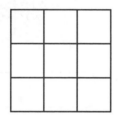 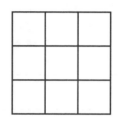 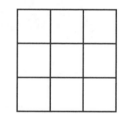

**c** $\frac{1}{4}$ turn anticlockwise

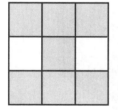 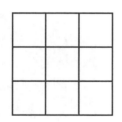 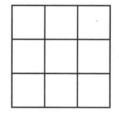 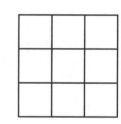

**d** $\frac{1}{2}$ turn anticlockwise

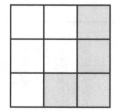 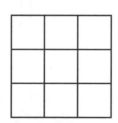 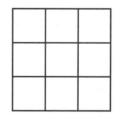 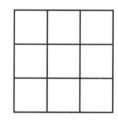

Make up your own turning pattern. What is your rule?

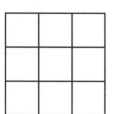 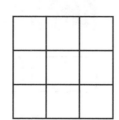 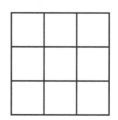

# Using number and place value

**1** Write these as numbers and words.

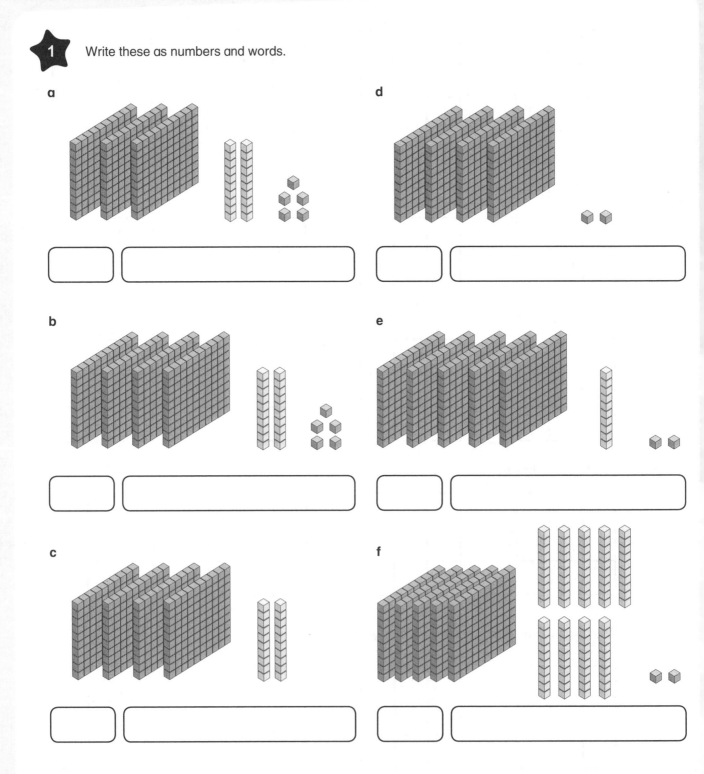

a

b

c

d

e

f

**2** Draw a line to match each group of words to the correct number.

eight hundred and sixty-five      658

five hundred and eighty-six      865

six hundred and eighty-five      856

eight hundred and fifty-six      685

six hundred and fifty-eight      586

**3** Write the number in words for each set of place-value cards.

a    4 0 0   9 0   1     [    ]

b   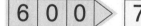 6 0 0   7 0     [    ]

c    5 0 0   5     [    ]

d    7 0 0   1 0   7     [    ]

e    9 0 0   9 0   9     [    ]

**4** Write the times shown on each clock face.

a

c

e

b

d

f

**5** Write the times shown on each clock face.

a

4 : 20

b

c

d

e

f  Which pair of clocks has the biggest time difference?

**6**  Draw hands on each clock to show the times.

Remember to draw the hour hand shorter than the minute hand.

a

8 : 35

c
7 : 25

e
11 : 07

b
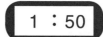

1 : 50

d
10 : 48

f
4 : 43

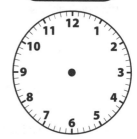

**7**  A clock runs slowly and loses 10 minutes every hour. If it is set at the correct time at 5:00 p.m., what time will the clock say in 4 hours' time?

Show the times every hour on these clocks.

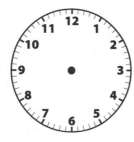

## 10b Using place value

**1** Answer these.

a How many minutes are in half an hour? [ minutes ]

b How many days are in 5 weeks? [ days ]

c How many months are in 2 years? [ months ]

d How many days are there in December? [ days ]

e How many seconds are in half a minute? [ seconds ]

**2** Circle the digit in each number that shows these values.

a Which digit shows ten?     **1**    **1**    **1**

b Which digit shows two hundred?     **2**    **2**    **2**

c Which digit shows thirty?     **3**    **3**    **3**

d Which digit shows four?     **4**    **4**    **4**

e Which digit shows five hundred?     **5**    **5**    **5**

f Which digit shows sixty?     **6**    **6**    **6**

**3** Write the numbers 100, 10 and 1 more than each of these.

a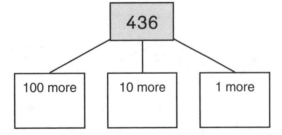

c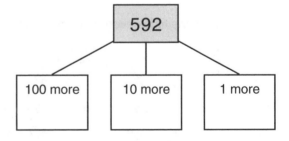

b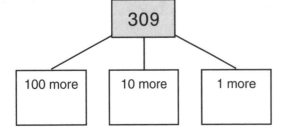

d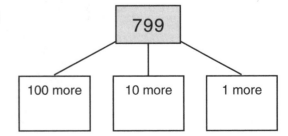

**4** Use these rods to partition these numbers in different ways.
Write the missing values.

| 350 |
|---|

**a**  350 = 300 + ☐

350 = 200 + ☐ + 50

350 = 100 + 100 + ☐ + 50

**b**  350 = ☐ + 50

350 = 300 + ☐ + 10

350 = 300 + 20 + ☐ + 10

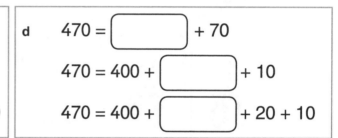

| 470 |
|---|

**c**  470 = 400 + ☐

470 = ☐ + 200 + 70

470 = 200 + 100 + ☐ + 70

**d**  470 = ☐ + 70

470 = 400 + ☐ + 10

470 = 400 + ☐ + 20 + 10

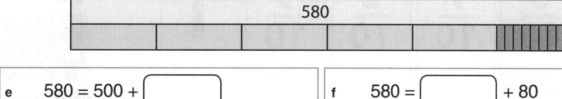

| 580 |
|---|

**e**  580 = 500 + ☐

580 = ☐ + 200 + 80

580 = 300 + ☐ + 100 + 80

**f**  580 = ☐ + 80

580 = 500 + ☐ + 10

580 = 500 + 40 + ☐ + 10

**5** Play this game in pairs.

**YOU WILL NEED:**
- **6 counters each**
- **set of 20 cards copied from these:**

| one-tenth | two-tenths | three-tenths | four-tenths | five-tenths |
|---|---|---|---|---|
| six-tenths | seven-tenths | eight-tenths | nine-tenths | one |

| $\frac{1}{10}$ | $\frac{2}{10}$ | $\frac{3}{10}$ | $\frac{4}{10}$ | $\frac{5}{10}$ |
|---|---|---|---|---|
| $\frac{6}{10}$ | $\frac{7}{10}$ | $\frac{8}{10}$ | $\frac{9}{10}$ | 1 |

**To play:**

- Shuffle the 20 cards and place them in a pile face down.
- Take turns to turn the top card over.
- Place a counter on the track to match the number card turned over.
- If there is already a counter on the number, replace it with your own counter.
- Once the 20 cards have been turned over, shuffle them and start from the top again.
- The winner is the first player to get 3 of their counters in a row.

# 3-digit sums and differences

 **1** Answer these.

a 5 + 8 = ☐

50 + 80 = ☐

57 + 80 = ☐

500 + 800 = ☐

570 + 800 = ☐

b 7 + 7 = ☐

70 + 70 = ☐

76 + 70 = ☐

700 + 700 = ☐

760 + 700 = ☐

c 9 + 6 = ☐

90 + 60 = ☐

94 + 60 = ☐

900 + 600 = ☐

940 + 600 = ☐

 **2**

**YOU WILL NEED:**
• Base 10 apparatus

Add these. Use Base 10 apparatus to help.

a 157 + 9 = ☐

b 167 + 8 = ☐

c 177 + 7 = ☐

d 187 + 6 = ☐

e 197 + 5 = ☐

f 207 + 4 = ☐

**3** Complete these total towers.

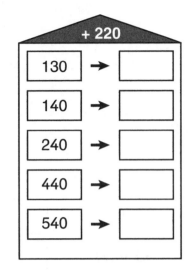

**a**

+ 220

| 130 | → | |
| 140 | → | |
| 240 | → | |
| 440 | → | |
| 540 | → | |

**b**

+ 330

| 110 | → | |
| 210 | → | |
| 420 | → | |
| 440 | → | |
| 540 | → | |

**c**

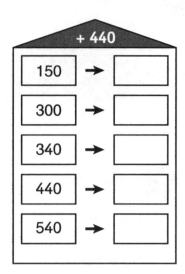

+ 440

| 150 | → | |
| 300 | → | |
| 340 | → | |
| 440 | → | |
| 540 | → | |

**4** Answer these.

**a**
```
    1  6  7
+   5  3  2
  _____
```

**b**
```
    6  2  5
+   2  4  5
  _____
```

**c**
```
    5  2  8
+   3  1  9
  _____
```

**d**
```
    3  6  0
+   5  4  3
  _____
```

**e**
```
    4  3  8
+   4  6  5
  _____
```

**f**
```
    2  9  7
+   8  0  8
  _____
```

**g**
```
    6  4  8
+   7  9  5
  _____
```

**h**
```
    8  7  5
+   4  6  7
  _____
```

**5** Complete this number puzzle.

| a | | b | | c | | d |
|---|---|---|---|---|---|---|
| | ▓ | e | | | ▓ | |
| f | | | ▓ | g | | |

### Across

- **a** 416 + 447
- **c** 324 + 503
- **e** 158 + 725
- **f** 308 + 238
- **g** 229 + 546

### Down

- **a** 435 + 370
- **b** 267 + 119
- **c** 356 + 481
- **d** 229 + 506

Working

---

**6** The digits 1 to 9 are missing from these additions.
Complete them with the digits in the correct places.

$$\begin{array}{r} \boxed{\phantom{0}}\,7\;5 \\ +\;6\,\boxed{\phantom{0}}\,4 \\ \hline 8\;\;0\,\boxed{\phantom{0}} \end{array}$$

$$\begin{array}{r} 2\;9\,\boxed{\phantom{0}} \\ +\;5\,\boxed{\phantom{0}}\,9 \\ \hline \boxed{\phantom{0}}\,4\;1 \end{array}$$

$$\begin{array}{r} 2\;9\,\boxed{\phantom{0}} \\ +\;3\,\boxed{\phantom{0}}\,4 \\ \hline \boxed{\phantom{0}}\,5\;1 \end{array}$$

**1** Answer these.

a  13 – 7 = ⬚

   130 – 70 = ⬚

   135 – 70 = ⬚

c  17 – 9 = ⬚

   170 – 90 = ⬚

   177 – 90 = ⬚

b  15 – 8 = ⬚

   150 – 80 = ⬚

   156 – 80 = ⬚

d  19 – 11 = ⬚

   190 – 110 = ⬚

   199 – 110 = ⬚

 **2** What is the difference between each pair of numbers?
Count on the number line to show your method.

a

247       683

Difference is ⬚

b

338       507

Difference is ⬚

c

294       675

Difference is ⬚

d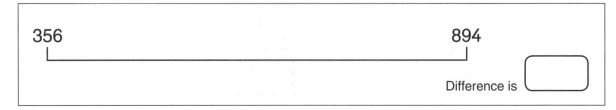

356       894

Difference is ⬚

**3**

Complete these. Use Base 10 apparatus to help.

| 100 | 10 | 1 |
|---|---|---|
| | | |

**a**

```
    4  8  7
 -  1  5  9
```

```
    7  2  3
 -  6  1  5
```

```
    9  6  2
 -  4  1  4
```

**b**

```
    5  4  9
 -  2  3  4
```

```
    6  4  7
 -  2  8  4
```

```
    9  4  6
 -  4  9  3
```

**c**

```
    4  1  6
 -  1  8  7
```

```
    5  6  3
 -  2  8  5
```

```
    9  3  1
 -  4  7  7
```

**d**

```
    4  0  6
 -  1  5  7
```

```
    7  0  3
 -  4  7  6
```

```
    9  0  5
 -  5  8  7
```

**4** A jug holds 985 ml of juice.
The juice is poured into four glasses in turn.
Write the amount left in the jug after each
glass has been filled.

Remember the next
glass is poured from
the amount that is left.

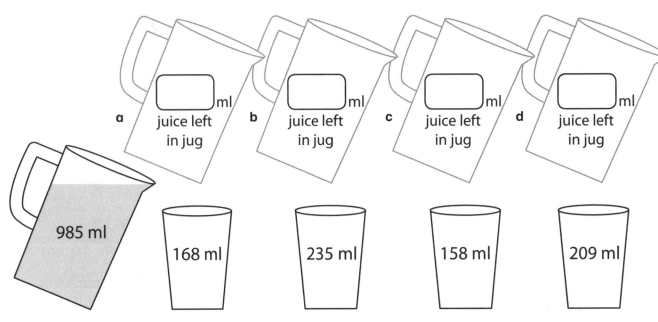

a ☐ ml
juice left
in jug

b ☐ ml
juice left
in jug

c ☐ ml
juice left
in jug

d ☐ ml
juice left
in jug

985 ml

168 ml    235 ml    158 ml    209 ml

**5** The digits 1 to 9 are missing from these subtractions.
Complete them with the digits in the correct place.

| 1 | 2 | 3 | 4 | 5 | 6 | 7 | 8 | 9 |
|---|---|---|---|---|---|---|---|---|

```
    7  6  5            ☐  0  3            5  4  ☐
 -  ☐  9  ☐         -  3  ☐  ☐        -  ☐  ☐  7
 _____        _____       _____
    1  ☐  3            2  8  4            1  5  7
```

# Representing whole numbers and fractions

**12a** **Representing whole numbers and tenths**

**1** What number is represented by each of these?

**a**

H T O

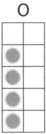

**b**

H T O

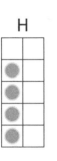

**c**

H T O

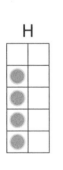

**d**

H T O

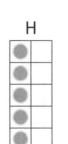

**e**

H T O

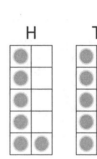

**f**

H T O

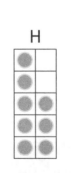

**YOU WILL NEED:**
• Base 10 apparatus

Use Base 10 apparatus to partition these numbers in different ways.
Write the missing values.

| Hundreds | Tens | Ones |
|---|---|---|

**a**  682 = 600 + [ ] + 2

682 = 500 + [ ] + 2

682 = 500 + 100 + [ ]

**b**  682 = 600 + 80 + [ ]

682 = 600 + [ ] + 12

682 = 500 + [ ] + 12

| Hundreds | Tens | Ones |
|---|---|---|

**c**  539 = 500 + [ ] + 9

539 = 400 + [ ] + 9

539 = 400 + 100 + [ ]

**d**  539 = 500 + 30 + [ ]

539 = 500 + [ ] + 19

539 = 400 + [ ] + 19

| Hundreds | Tens | Ones |
|---|---|---|

**e**  746 = 700 + [ ] + 6

746 = 600 + [ ] + 6

746 = 600 + 100 + [ ]

**f**  746 = 700 + 40 + [ ]

746 = 700 + [ ] + 16

746 = 600 + [ ] + 16

This shows $1\frac{2}{10}$.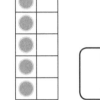

Write the fraction shown for each of these.

**a**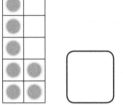

**e**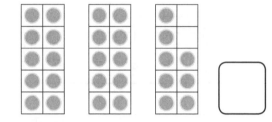

**b**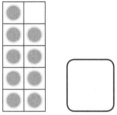

**f**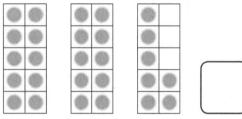

**c**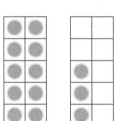

**g**

**d**

**h**

**4** Look at this number line. Write the number for each arrow.

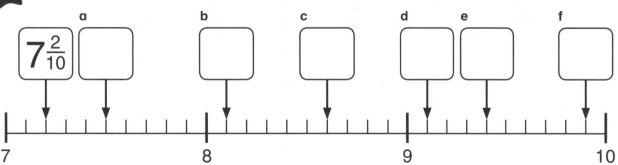

**5** Tenths are used for measuring in centimetres. This nail is $3\frac{4}{10}$ cm long.

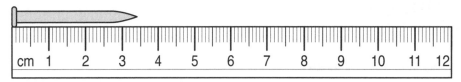

Write the length of each nail.

a

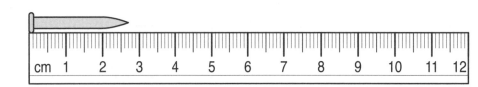

b

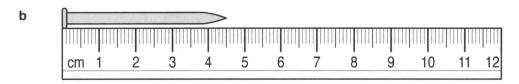

c

d

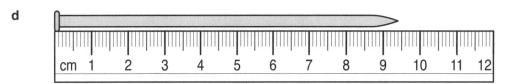

e

| Nail | Whole centimetres | Tenths of a centimetre |
|---|---|---|
| Example | 3 | $\frac{4}{10}$ |
| a | | |
| b | | |
| c | | |
| d | | |
| e | | |

**1** Write each fraction shaded.

Are they more or less than $\frac{1}{2}$? Write 'more' or 'less' in each space.

**a**

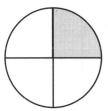

⬜ is ⬜ than $\frac{1}{2}$.

**b**

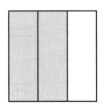

⬜ is ⬜ than $\frac{1}{2}$.

**c**

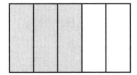

⬜ is ⬜ than $\frac{1}{2}$.

**d**

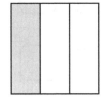

⬜ is ⬜ than $\frac{1}{2}$.

**e**

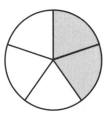

⬜ is ⬜ than $\frac{1}{2}$.

**f**

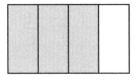

⬜ is ⬜ than $\frac{1}{2}$.

**2** Use the fraction wall to help answer these.

| 1 whole | | | | | | | |
|---|---|---|---|---|---|---|---|
| $\frac{1}{2}$ | | | | $\frac{1}{2}$ | | | |
| $\frac{1}{3}$ | | $\frac{1}{3}$ | | | $\frac{1}{3}$ | | |
| $\frac{1}{4}$ | | $\frac{1}{4}$ | | $\frac{1}{4}$ | | $\frac{1}{4}$ | |
| $\frac{1}{6}$ | $\frac{1}{6}$ | $\frac{1}{6}$ | | $\frac{1}{6}$ | $\frac{1}{6}$ | | $\frac{1}{6}$ |
| $\frac{1}{8}$ | $\frac{1}{8}$ | $\frac{1}{8}$ | $\frac{1}{8}$ | $\frac{1}{8}$ | $\frac{1}{8}$ | $\frac{1}{8}$ | $\frac{1}{8}$ |

**a** Which is larger $\frac{1}{2}$ or $\frac{1}{4}$? ◻

**b** Which is larger $\frac{1}{8}$ or $\frac{1}{6}$? ◻

**c** Which is larger $\frac{1}{3}$ or $\frac{1}{4}$? ◻

**d** Which is larger $\frac{1}{2}$ or $\frac{1}{8}$? ◻

**e** Which is larger $\frac{1}{4}$ or $\frac{1}{8}$? ◻

**f** Which is larger $\frac{1}{6}$ or $\frac{1}{3}$? ◻

**3** Write the missing < or > to make each sentence true.
Use the fraction wall to help you.

**a** $\frac{1}{2}$ ◻ $\frac{3}{4}$

**c** $\frac{2}{6}$ ◻ $\frac{2}{8}$

**e** $\frac{3}{8}$ ◻ $\frac{2}{6}$

**b** $\frac{1}{6}$ ◻ $\frac{2}{3}$

**d** $\frac{3}{4}$ ◻ $\frac{4}{6}$

**f** $\frac{2}{3}$ ◻ $\frac{3}{6}$

**4** Look at the fraction of each circle shaded.
Write these fractions in order starting with the smallest.

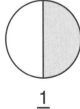     

$\frac{1}{2}$ $\frac{1}{4}$ $\frac{2}{3}$ $\frac{1}{3}$ $\frac{3}{4}$ $\frac{1}{6}$

     ◻

smallest ➡              ➡ largest

**5** Answer these. Use the fraction bars to help you.

**a** $\frac{1}{3}$ of 15 = ◯

| 15 | | |
|---|---|---|
| $\frac{1}{3}$ | | |

**b** $\frac{1}{5}$ of 15 = ◯

| 15 | | | | |
|---|---|---|---|---|
| $\frac{1}{5}$ | | | | |

**c** $\frac{1}{4}$ of 24 = ◯

| 24 | | | |
|---|---|---|---|
| $\frac{1}{4}$ | | | |

**d** $\frac{1}{6}$ of 24 = ◯

| 24 | | | | | |
|---|---|---|---|---|---|
| $\frac{1}{6}$ | | | | | |

**e** $\frac{1}{10}$ of 30 = ◯

| 30 | | | | | | | | | |
|---|---|---|---|---|---|---|---|---|---|
| $\frac{1}{10}$ | | | | | | | | | |

**f** $\frac{1}{3}$ of 30 = ◯

| 30 | | |
|---|---|---|
| $\frac{1}{3}$ | | |

**6** Work out the number of each farm animal owned by these farmers.

**a** Rob has a total of 24 farm animals.

$\frac{1}{2}$ are chickens

$\frac{1}{4}$ are ducks

$\frac{1}{6}$ are cows

The rest of his animals are horses.

How many of each animal does he have?

chickens

ducks

cows

horses

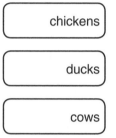

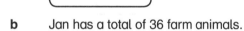

**b** Jan has a total of 36 farm animals.

$\frac{1}{3}$ are sheep

$\frac{1}{4}$ are turkeys

$\frac{1}{6}$ are chickens

$\frac{1}{9}$ are cows

The rest of her animals are pigs.

How many of each animal does he have?

sheep

turkeys

chickens

cows

pigs

Colour $\frac{1}{2}$ of each circle. Write the equivalent fractions you have shaded.

**YOU WILL NEED:**
- coloured pencils

**a**

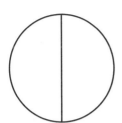

$\frac{1}{2} = \dfrac{\square}{\square}$

**c**

$\frac{1}{2} = \dfrac{\square}{\square}$

**e**

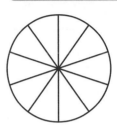

$\frac{1}{2} = \dfrac{\square}{\square}$

**b**

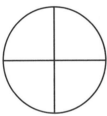

$\frac{1}{2} = \dfrac{\square}{\square}$

**d**

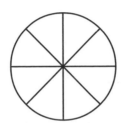

$\frac{1}{2} = \dfrac{\square}{\square}$

**f**

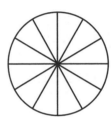

$\frac{1}{2} = \dfrac{\square}{\square}$

 Circle the rectangle that shows an equivalent fraction to these.

Write the equivalent fraction.

**a**

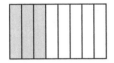  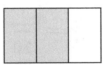 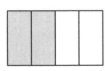

$\dfrac{\square}{\square} = \dfrac{1}{2}$

**b**

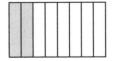 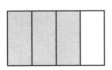 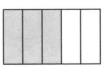 

$\dfrac{\square}{\square} = \dfrac{1}{4}$

**c**

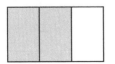 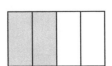 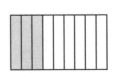 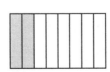

$\dfrac{\square}{\square} = \dfrac{1}{3}$

**d**

 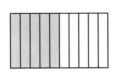 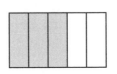 

$\dfrac{\square}{\square} = \dfrac{1}{5}$

**3** Look at the fractions that are shaded. Write each fraction in 2 ways.

**a**

$$\frac{\boxed{\phantom{0}}}{\boxed{\phantom{0}}} = \frac{\boxed{\phantom{0}}}{\boxed{\phantom{0}}}$$

**b**

$$\frac{\boxed{\phantom{0}}}{\boxed{\phantom{0}}} = \frac{\boxed{\phantom{0}}}{\boxed{\phantom{0}}}$$

**c**

$$\frac{\boxed{\phantom{0}}}{\boxed{\phantom{0}}} = \frac{\boxed{\phantom{0}}}{\boxed{\phantom{0}}}$$

**d**

$$\frac{\boxed{\phantom{0}}}{\boxed{\phantom{0}}} = \frac{\boxed{\phantom{0}}}{\boxed{\phantom{0}}}$$

 **4** Shade each rectangle to help you add these fractions.

**a**

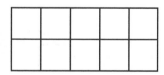

$$\frac{1}{5} + \frac{3}{5} = \frac{\boxed{\phantom{0}}}{5}$$

**b**

$$\frac{3}{10} + \frac{5}{10} = \frac{\boxed{\phantom{0}}}{10}$$

**c**

$$\frac{1}{8} + \frac{5}{8} = \frac{\boxed{\phantom{0}}}{8}$$

**d**

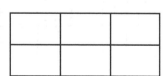

$$\frac{1}{6} + \frac{4}{6} = \frac{\boxed{\phantom{0}}}{6}$$

**5** Answer these.

a   $\dfrac{1}{5} + \dfrac{1}{5} =$ ☐

   $\dfrac{1}{8} + \dfrac{1}{8} =$ ☐

   $\dfrac{1}{9} + \dfrac{1}{9} =$ ☐

c   $\dfrac{3}{6} + \dfrac{2}{6} =$ ☐

   $\dfrac{3}{7} + \dfrac{2}{7} =$ ☐

   $\dfrac{3}{8} + \dfrac{2}{8} =$ ☐

b   $\dfrac{3}{10} - \dfrac{1}{10} =$ ☐

   $\dfrac{3}{5} - \dfrac{1}{5} =$ ☐

   $\dfrac{3}{4} - \dfrac{1}{4} =$ ☐

d   $\dfrac{7}{8} - \dfrac{4}{8} =$ ☐

   $\dfrac{5}{8} - \dfrac{3}{8} =$ ☐

   $\dfrac{3}{8} - \dfrac{2}{8} =$ ☐

**6** Make a set of fraction families for $\dfrac{1}{10}$ kg.

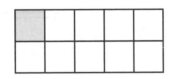  

Write 6 different equivalent weights. What do you notice about the fractions?

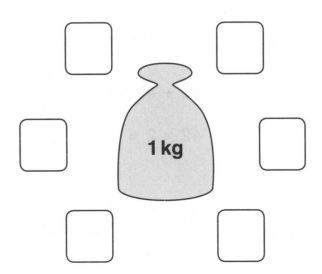

**13a**  Towards the written method for multiplication

 **1**  Answer these.

a   2 × 2 = ☐

20 × 2 = ☐

40 × 2 = ☐

80 × 2 = ☐

b   2 × 4 = ☐

20 × 4 = ☐

40 × 4 = ☐

80 × 4 = ☐

c   2 × 6 = ☐

20 × 6 = ☐

40 × 6 = ☐

80 × 6 = ☐

d   2 × 8 = ☐

20 × 8 = ☐

40 × 8 = ☐

80 × 8 = ☐

 **2**

**YOU WILL NEED:**
• **counters**
• **ten frames**

Complete these. Use counters and ten frames to help you.

a
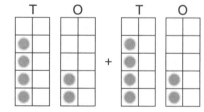

42 + 42 = ☐

42 × 2 = ☐

b
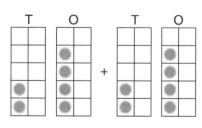

24 + 24 = ☐

24 × 2 = ☐

**c**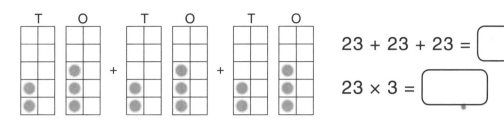

$23 + 23 + 23 =$ ⬚

$23 \times 3 =$ ⬚

**d**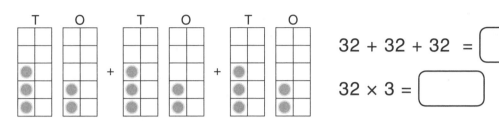

$32 + 32 + 32 =$ ⬚

$32 \times 3 =$ ⬚

**e**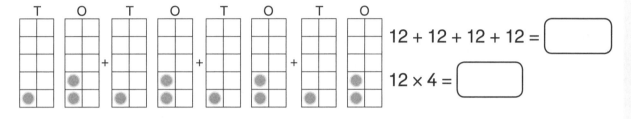

$12 + 12 + 12 + 12 =$ ⬚

$12 \times 4 =$ ⬚

**f**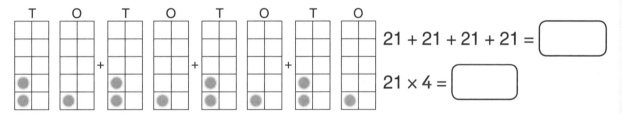

$21 + 21 + 21 + 21 =$ ⬚

$21 \times 4 =$ ⬚

⭐ **3**   Answer these.

**a**   $24 \times 3 \rightarrow 20 \times 3 =$ ⬚

$4 \times 3 =$ ⬚ $+$

$\overline{\phantom{4 \times 3}}$

$24 \times 3 =$ ⬚

**b**   $24 \times 4 \rightarrow 20 \times 4 =$ ⬚

$4 \times 4 =$ ⬚ $+$

$\overline{\phantom{4 \times 4}}$

$24 \times 4 =$ ⬚

**c**   $24 \times 5 \rightarrow 20 \times 5 =$ ⬚

$4 \times 5 =$ ⬚ $+$

$\overline{\phantom{4 \times 5}}$

$24 \times 5 =$ ⬚

**d**   $24 \times 6 \rightarrow 20 \times 6 =$ ⬚

$4 \times 6 =$ ⬚ $+$

$\overline{\phantom{4 \times 6}}$

$24 \times 6 =$ ⬚

**4** Complete these.

$18 \times 2 =$ ☐ 36 ☐   ×   10   8

2   | 20 | 16 | → 20 + 16 = 36

**a** $16 \times 3 =$ ☐   ×   10   6

3   ☐☐   → ☐ + ☐ = ☐

**b** $25 \times 5 =$ ☐   ×   20   5

5   ☐☐   → ☐ + ☐ = ☐

**c** $39 \times 2 =$ ☐   ×   30   9

2   ☐☐   → ☐ + ☐ = ☐

**d** $43 \times 4 =$ ☐   ×   40   3

4   ☐☐   → ☐ + ☐ = ☐

**e** $57 \times 2 =$ ☐   ×   50   7

2   ☐☐   → ☐ + ☐ = ☐

**f** $36 \times 5 =$ ☐   ×   30   6

5   ☐☐   → ☐ + ☐ = ☐

**5** Answer these. Show your working out using the written method.

$18 \times 2 = \boxed{36}$

$$\begin{array}{r} 1\ 8 \\ \times\quad 2 \\ \hline 1\ 6 \\ 2\ 0 \\ \hline 3\ 6 \\ \hline \end{array}$$

**a** $16 \times 3 = \boxed{\phantom{00}}$

$$\begin{array}{r} 1\ 6 \\ \times\quad 3 \\ \hline \\ \hline \\ \hline \end{array}$$

**d** $43 \times 4 = \boxed{\phantom{00}}$

$$\begin{array}{r} 4\ 3 \\ \times\quad 4 \\ \hline \\ \hline \\ \hline \end{array}$$

**b** $25 \times 5 = \boxed{\phantom{00}}$

$$\begin{array}{r} 2\ 5 \\ \times\quad 5 \\ \hline \\ \hline \\ \hline \end{array}$$

**e** $57 \times 2 = \boxed{\phantom{00}}$

$$\begin{array}{r} 5\ 7 \\ \times\quad 2 \\ \hline \\ \hline \\ \hline \end{array}$$

**c** $39 \times 2 = \boxed{\phantom{00}}$

$$\begin{array}{r} 3\ 9 \\ \times\quad 2 \\ \hline \\ \hline \\ \hline \end{array}$$

**f** $36 \times 5 = \boxed{\phantom{00}}$

$$\begin{array}{r} 3\ 6 \\ \times\quad 5 \\ \hline \\ \hline \\ \hline \end{array}$$

Compare the methods for questions 4 and 5.

What is the same and what is different about each method?

**6** Answer these. Choose a method for working out each answer.

a $38 \times 5 =$ [ ]

b $26 \times 3 =$ [ ]

c $54 \times 2 =$ [ ]

d $46 \times 4 =$ [ ]

 **7** Read and answer these.

a A minibus holds 14 passengers. How many people will 4 buses hold? [ ] people

b Mr Jones travels 28 km each day to and from work. He works 5 days a week.

How far does he travel altogether in a week? [ ] km

c A market stall has 4 crates of coconuts. There are 28 coconuts in a crate.

How many coconuts are there in total? [ ] coconuts

d A farmer fills 3 trays of eggs. Each tray holds 36 eggs.

How many eggs does the farmer have? [ ] eggs

e The battery in a mobile phone lasts for 7 days.

How many hours does the battery last? [ ] hours

f Phone calls cost 49p per minute. How much will a 3 minute phone call cost? [ ] p

**8** Use digit cards or write the digits 2, 3 and 4 on small squares of paper.

**YOU WILL NEED:**
• digit cards

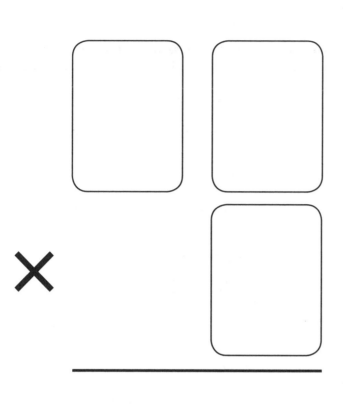

**a** How many different answers can you make?

**b** What is the largest answer you can make?

**c** What is the smallest answer you can make?

**d** Which multiplication gives you the answer nearest to 100?

Use the number line to answer the questions.

1 2 3 4 5 6 7 8 9 10 11 12 13 14 15 16 17 18 19 20 21 22 23 24 25 26 27 28 29 30 31 32 33 34 35 36

**a** How many 2s in 36?

$36 \div 2 = $ ⬚

**b** How many 3s in 36?

$36 \div 3 = $ ⬚

**c** How many 4s in 36?

$36 \div 4 = $ ⬚

**d** How many 6s in 36?

$36 \div 6 = $ ⬚

**e** How many 9s in 36?

$36 \div 9 = $ ⬚

**f** How many 12s in 36?

$36 \div 12 = $ ⬚

 Complete these for each array.

**a**

5

3 | ⬚⬚⬚⬚⬚

$3 \times 5 = $ ⬚

$5 \times 3 = $ ⬚

$15 \div 5 = $ ⬚

$15 \div 3 = $ ⬚

**c**

6

4 | ⬚⬚⬚⬚⬚⬚

$4 \times 6 = $ ⬚

$6 \times 4 = $ ⬚

$24 \div 6 = $ ⬚

$24 \div 4 = $ ⬚

**b**

6

3 | ⬚⬚⬚⬚⬚⬚

$3 \times 6 = $ ⬚

$6 \times 3 = $ ⬚

$18 \div 3 = $ ⬚

$18 \div 6 = $ ⬚

**d**

6

5 | ⬚⬚⬚⬚⬚⬚

$6 \times 5 = $ ⬚

$5 \times 6 = $ ⬚

$30 \div 5 = $ ⬚

$30 \div 6 = $ ⬚

**e**

12

5

$12 \times 5 =$ ☐

$5 \times 12 =$ ☐

$60 \div 5 =$ ☐

$60 \div 12 =$ ☐

**f**

12

6

$12 \times 6 =$ ☐

$6 \times 12 =$ ☐

$72 \div 6 =$ ☐

$72 \div 12 =$ ☐

**3**  Complete the facts for each of these.

**a**

20

4        5

$4 \times$ ☐ $=$ ☐

☐ $\times 4 =$ ☐

☐ $\div 4 =$ ☐

☐ $\div$ ☐ $= 4$

**c**

45

9        5

$5 \times$ ☐ $=$ ☐

☐ $\times 5 =$ ☐

☐ $\div 5 =$ ☐

☐ $\div$ ☐ $= 5$

**b**

28

4        7

$4 \times$ ☐ $=$ ☐

☐ $\times 4 =$ ☐

☐ $\div 4 =$ ☐

☐ $\div$ ☐ $= 4$

**d**

55

5        11

$5 \times$ ☐ $=$ ☐

☐ $\times 5 =$ ☐

☐ $\div 5 =$ ☐

☐ $\div$ ☐ $= 5$

**4** Complete these.
Use Base 10 apparatus to help you.

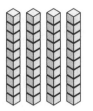 

**YOU WILL NEED:**
• Base 10 apparatus

**a**
4 | 5 2

**c**
3 | 5 4

**e**
4 | 6 0

**b**
5 | 6 5

**d**
2 | 5 6

**f**
3 | 7 2

**5**   Answer these problems.

**a**   18 balloons are given to a group of 3 children. They divide the balloons equally between them.

How many balloons does each child have? [ _____ balloons ]

**b**   48 daffodils are planted in a border. There are 6 equal rows of daffodils.

How many daffodils are in each row? [ _____ daffodils ]

**c**   A baker made 36 gingerbread men. How many boxes would he need to put 3 gingerbread

men in each box? [ _____ boxes ]

**d**   A farmer has 84 eggs from his chickens. How many boxes does he need if each box

holds 6 eggs? [ _____ boxes ]

**6**   True or false?
45 can be divided exactly by 3.

How can you prove your answer?

**14a** All about 2-D shapes

**1** Write the names of these shapes.

a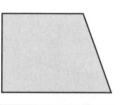

b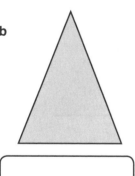

c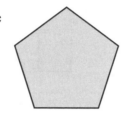

d

e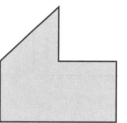

f

g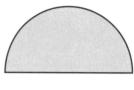

h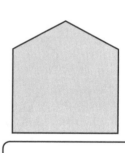

**2** Sort the shapes in question 1 onto this Venn diagram.

Write the letters in the correct areas.

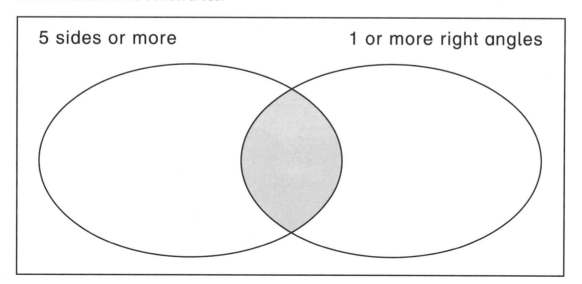

5 sides or more        1 or more right angles

**3** Tick the shapes that are symmetrical.

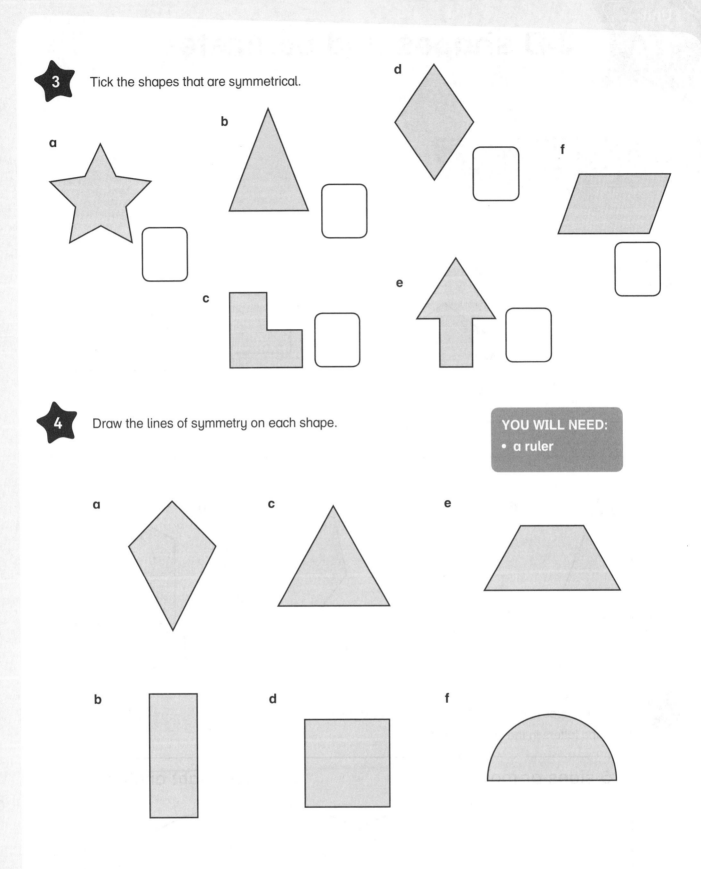

a

b

c

d

e

f

**4** Draw the lines of symmetry on each shape.

YOU WILL NEED:
• a ruler

a

b

c

d

e

f

**5** These are sketches of shapes so the lengths are not accurate.

Use a ruler and pencil to draw each shape accurately.

YOU WILL NEED:
• a ruler

**a**

A       B

D    5 cm    C

**b**

A       B    4 cm

D   8 cm   C

**c**

A       B    3 cm

D   6 cm   C

**d**

A       B

D   3 cm   C

YOU WILL NEED:
• card or paper
• scissors

**6** This triangle is half a shape. It can make these different whole shapes.

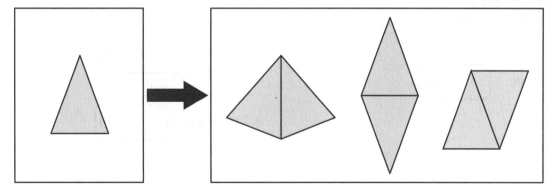

**a** Choose a triangle or quadrilateral. Copy it twice onto card or paper.

Cut out the shapes. Arrange them side to side to make different shapes.

**b** Sort the shapes you have made.

Which shapes have right angles? Which shapes have 4 sides?

**1** Calculate the perimeter of each shape.

**a**

8 cm

Perimeter = [ ] cm

**d**

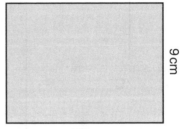

9 cm

12 cm

Perimeter = [ ] cm

**b**

4 cm

6 cm

Perimeter = [ ] cm

**e**

15 cm

Perimeter = [ ] cm

**c**

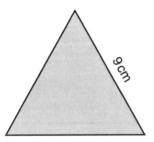

9 cm

Perimeter = [ ] cm

**f**

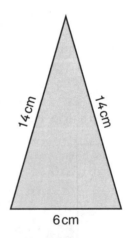

14 cm   14 cm

6 cm

Perimeter = [ ] cm

**2** Which shape has the greatest perimeter?

**a**

6 cm

9 cm

Perimeter = ____ cm

**c**

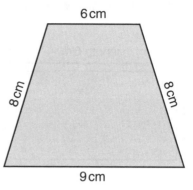

6 cm

8 cm    8 cm

9 cm

Perimeter = ____ cm

**b**

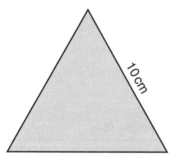

10 cm

Perimeter = ____ cm

**d**

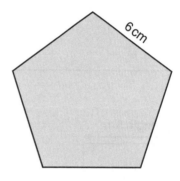

6 cm

Perimeter = ____ cm

The shape with the greatest perimeter is ____

**3** Calculate the perimeter of each shape.

**a**

3 cm

4 cm

Perimeter = ____ cm

**c**

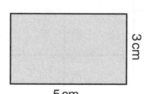

3 cm

5 cm

Perimeter = ____ cm

**e**

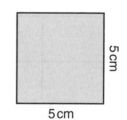

5 cm

5 cm

Perimeter = ____ cm

**b**

4 cm

4 cm

Perimeter = ____ cm

**d**

2 cm

6 cm

Perimeter = ____ cm

**f**

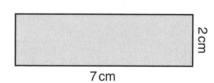

2 cm

7 cm

Perimeter = ____ cm

**121**

Complete this chart. Write the length and width of each rectangle and calculate the perimeter.

**a**

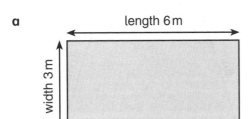

length 6 m · width 3 m

**d**

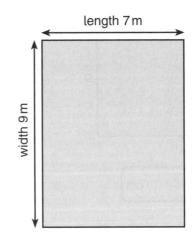

length 7 m · width 9 m

**b**

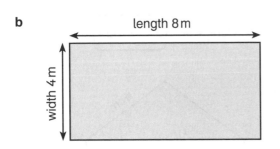

length 8 m · width 4 m

**c**

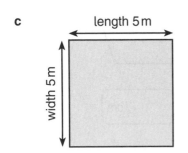

length 5 m · width 5 m

**e**

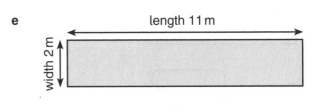

length 11 m · width 2 m

| Rectangle | Length | Add | Width | Total | Multiply by 2 | Perimeter |
|---|---|---|---|---|---|---|
| a | m | + | m | = m | m × 2 = | m |
| b | m | + | m | = m | m × 2 = | m |
| c | m | + | m | = m | m × 2 = | m |
| d | m | + | m | = m | m × 2 = | m |
| e | m | + | m | = m | m × 2 = | m |

**5** Draw 3 different shapes with the same perimeter as this square.

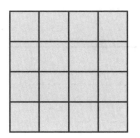

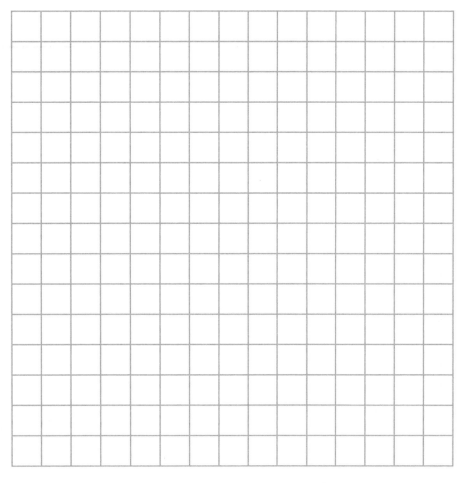

**6** Measure the perimeter of these shapes.

**YOU WILL NEED:**
• a ruler

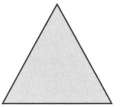

Perimeter = [          ] cm

Perimeter = [          ] cm

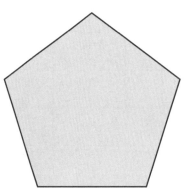

Perimeter = [          ] cm

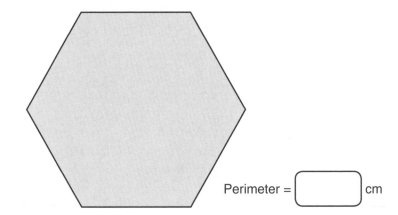

Perimeter = [          ] cm

What do you notice?

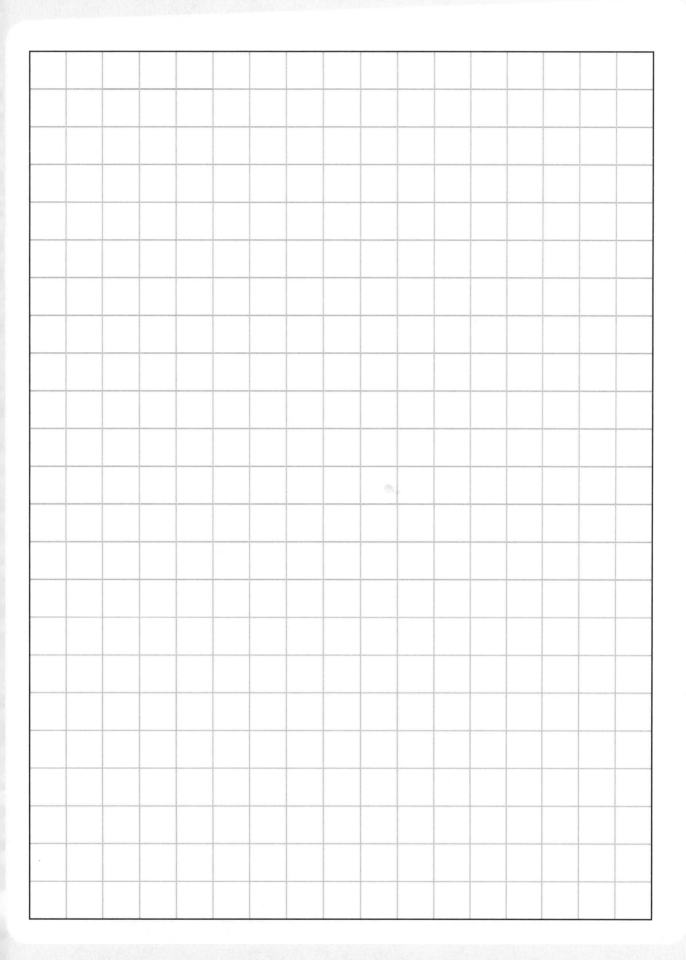